POLITICAL ANALYSIS THROUGH THE PRINCE SYSTEM

by

William D. Coplin

and

Michael K. O'Leary

LEARNING PACKAGES IN THE POLICY SCIENCES
PS-23

P Policy
S Studies
A Associates

P. O. Box 337
Croton-on-Hudson, NY 10520

ISBN 0-936826-18-5

TO THE INSTRUCTOR AND STUDENTS
ON THE OBJECTIVES AND MATERIALS:

THE PRIMARY OBJECTIVE:

This learning package will provide you with the information necessary to use the Prince System in making political forecasts and formulating political strategies.

UPON COMPLETION OF THIS PACKAGE, YOU WILL BE ABLE TO:

* Identify political issues that the Prince System can help you understand.

* Determine the information you need to make a political forecast about any political issue.

* Calculate the probabilities that a political decision will be taken.

* Identify strategies that could be used to change the probabilities in the desired direction.

THE FOLLOWING IS RECOMMENDED:

This package is adapted from Everyman's PRINCE: A Guide to Understanding Your Political Problems (North Scituate, Mass.: Duxbury Publishing Company, 1976. Revised edition). Although now out of print, the book should be carried by your college or university library.

TIME SPAN:

Two to three weeks.

TABLE OF CONTENTS

LISTING OF TABLES

CHAPTER 1: KNOWING WHEN TO USE THE PRINCE SYSTEM

The Prince System is a formula for gathering and analyzing information about any situation in which a decision will be made involving two or more people. The Prince System is like an accounting system. Just as an accountant uses his formulas to determine the status of a business operation, the user of the Prince System can determine the status of a decision that is about to be made (or rejected). By following the steps in the formula, you can make a prediction of how likely the decision is to be made, to be rejected, or to continue as an unresolved controversy. Perhaps even more important, the use of the Prince System helps you choose strategies that will enable you to change the situation more to your liking. If it is a decision you want made, you can make it more likely to happen; if you want to block the decision, you can help assure its defeat.

A. Who Has Used the Prince System

Since its development in the early 1970s, the Prince System has been used in every conceivable situation where collective decisions are made. To give you an idea of the range and flexibility of the Prince System, here are some examples of the uses that we have heard about:

- A parent blocked a school district decision that would have undermined the quality of education in his district. The school district wanted to combine the administration of an elementary school and a middle school. The parent felt that this decision would jeopardize the needs of the younger elementary school children. The school district presented impressive facts and figures about the wisdom of the proposed move. Although the administration had full authority to make the move (and in fact announced the decisions as final), the parent was able to use the Prince System to block the action.

- The Central Intelligence Agency predicted the outcome of an international conference. In 1979, a major international conference was held to set worldwide rules for telecommunications. Two years before the conference, the CIA was charged with predicting the outcome of the major decisions to be made at the conference. Using the Prince System, the CIA gathered information about which decisions were most likely to be approved at the conference. The predictions were used as a guide to diplomatic negotiations before and during the conference. As a result, the outcome was much more favorable to the United States than most observers had anticipated.

- A social worker got a neighborhood health center approved. Although funds were available for its construction, a badly needed local health center looked dead because of opposition by residents in the area where it would be built. A social worker who saw the necessity of the center used the Prince System to work with the minority in the area who approved it, as well as others in the city who favored the center, to create a political force that was able to get the center built.

- An office manager got his company to purchase a cost-effective computer system. The manager realized that his company was about to purchase a computer system that was much more expensive and complicated than his firm actually needed. Although the high-cost system was supported by the Data Analysis Supervisor who had much more technical expertise than the manager, the manager was nevertheless able to use the Prince System to work with others to block the initial purchase and bring about the purchase of a much less expensive and more appropriate system.

- A police chief got his city council to finance educational benefits for members of his force. The chief, in a large city, realized that an improved professional police force required increasing the educational benefits available to his officers. He wanted the city council to add these educational benefits to his budget. Although this was an unprecedented request ("why do police have to be sent to school?" most council members asked), the chief used the Prince System to involve enough council members and their constituents behind the proposal so that it eventually became a regular program in the police department.

- Chief executive officers of American businesses successfully predicted the passage of the Kemp-Roth tax cuts months before it happened. In early 1981, there was a great deal of doubt whether the Kemp-Roth tax cut would really be voted into law, in light of substantial opposition among Democrats in Congress. Chief executive

officers of several businesses used the Prince System
to forecast whether this important measure would actually
pass or be defeated -- vital information for businesses
which were trying to forecast its finances. The results
of this study, reported in the Summer 1981 issue of
Chief Executive Magazine, correctly forecast the passage
of the tax cut.

- Senior-level executives and international bankers predicted a sharp decline in interest rates during 1982.
In late 1981, economic forecasters were arguing about
whether interest rates (then around 20%) would stay at
that level, or possibly drop one or two points. A group
of business executives and international bankers used
the Prince System to predict the average prime rate for
all of 1982. The conclusion was that the prime rate
would fall below 15%, which it did.

- The Army Corps of Engineers improved its public involvement program. The Corps is frequently responsible for
construction projects that generate a lot of hostility
and opposition among landowners, conservationists, and
others who dislike the development projects the Corps
is engaged in. Many times public opposition forces a
radical modification, or even cancellation of a project
that is already under way. Some local Corps offices
have begun to use the Prince System to predict the support and opposition for planned projects. They also use
the system as the basis for public groups expressing
themselves on which parts of various projects they most
oppose, and which they didn't object to. As a result,
the Corps is able to tailor projects to satisfy the most
heavily involved groups at an early stage when such
modification is much less costly.

- The State Department predicted the outcome of upcoming
international negotiations. In the early 1970s, there
was much talk about the possibility of serious negotiations between North and South Korea over a series of
issues that could lead to greater exchanges between the
two countries. Officials of the U.S. State Department
produced a forecast of the outcome of these negotiations
using the Prince System. The system accurately predicted
that no agreement would be reached except for one decision -- an increase in the exchange of mail between the
two countries.

- A major money-center bank improved its overseas reporting.
The bank had trouble analyzing the reports of its overseas offices which were supposed to provide objective
assessments about the desirability of loans in each

country. The reports from different offices covered
very different topics and were therefore almost impossible to compare. Furthermore, bank headquarters suspected
that overseas offices frequently became much too friendly and uncritical about the country in which they were
operating. So headquarters began to have all overseas
offices use the Prince System as the basis for gathering
and reporting information on each country. As a result,
headquarters much improved its ability to compare countries, and also to evaluate the objectivity of the reports from the field.

- A sales manager improved his sales forecasting. The
  manager, working in a major manufacturing company, regu-
  larly had his salesmen report the probabilities that
  each of their potential customers would make a major
  purchase. The manager realized that these "probabilities" were, in fact, nothing but guesses expressed in
  numerical terms. The manager began having his salesmen
  use the Prince System as the basis for their probability
  forecasts. As a result, it became possible for the sales
  force and the manager to make much more confident con-
  clusions about who the best prospects were. They were
  therefore able to spend much more time on the best prospects, substantially improving the efficiency of their
  sales efforts.

In all of these uses of the Prince System, someone was
trying to get a decision made by getting more influential
people supporting than opposing the decision. In short, they
sought to build a winning coalition that would lead to the
decision they wanted. Figuring out how to build a winning
coalition is tricky; helping you to do so is what this learning package is about. The single most important difficulty
in building a winning coalition is the failure to see the
need for such a coalition, or prematurely resigning yourself
to the conclusion that getting one is impossible. These
attitudes are unfortunate and self-defeating because they
will keep you from achieving your goals.

B.   More Things Are Political Than You Think

Building a winning coalition sounds suspiciously as if
we are discussing politics. It is true that the Prince System, which is the method we will use to show you how to build
a winning coalition, was developed and originally used by the
government. And it has been mostly used by bureaucrats,
politicians, and interest groups to help them get agreement
from other bureaucrats, politicians, and interest groups.

But it is important to understand that the need for winning coalitions is much more widespread than governmental politics. Many areas of daily life, which are almost never thought of as "political," actually require the creation of a winning coalition for success. Creating a winning coalition is needed in order to get a raise, to buy a new family car, to convince the Little League to schedule fewer games on Sunday afternoons, or to convince a customer to make a big purchase from you.

Succeeding in all of these, and hundreds of other day-to-day goals doesn't involve the drama and hoopla of what we usually associate with government and politics. However, the politics as portrayed in newspapers and television is similar to the politics of daily life because essentially the same task is required -- building a winning coalition. The setting and stakes are very different, but the underlying process is the same. Accepting this similarity is a big step along the road to happiness.

Whenever you need agreement among influential people to make a decision that you want, your only choice is to find out how to build a winning coalition. This bothers many people because at the very least it is time-consuming. Even worse, it is frequently costly. It costs in self-esteem if you think that you have the right to make the decision without going through all the trouble. It also costs in future obligations that you incur in order to get the necessary agreement.

In our increasingly fragmented society, more and more decisions are made through the creation (and disintegration) of winning coalitions. Even in formal organizations where authority is "officially" held by one person -- the boss, the school principal -- few decisions are really made by a single person.

Consider the president, placed at the apex of the American political structure. People sometimes talk about the members of a president's administration as a "family," which is an unintentionally telling metaphor. Every presidential administration is indeed a family -- squabbling, fighting, demanding, recalcitrant, and disobedient. The only way the president, despite his authority, can get things done is to work like a harrassed father, to build new winning coalitions for all the different things he is trying to accomplish.

Look at how our presidents have talked about authority and compare it to what they have actually done to make themselves successful in office. The first thing to notice is that they all act as if they were in control. President

Harry Truman liked to boast that "the buck stops here." The record shows that Truman, like every other president, had to work very hard to build winning coalitions to accomplish his goals.

Most people in authority recognize that decisions are rarely made by single individuals regardless of their title. In a large organization if you ask your boss for a raise, he will need to get the support of his bosses. He will also talk to other bosses about what their salary policies are, and discuss with other subordinates how they feel about raises for others. In a smaller company, the boss is probably the president. But even in this case the complete formal authority about raises and the like is not matched by actual practice. The top person is likely to be sensitive to the views of other workers, and his or her spouse. Other people who are also likely to be consulted are the boss's accountant and banker.

For those of us not in authority, it is important to remember that the idea of complete authority is a myth. No matter how complete the ruler's authority appears to be, his decisions are shaped by others. You may want to believe the myth and forget the reality because it relieves you of the need to do anything about a decision you don't like and allows you to avoid a conflict. If you believe in the myth of authority, a boss's decision is final, whether you like it or not. If, on the other hand, you accept the reality of the constant possibility of creating winning coalitions, then no decision is ever final, which gives you the opportunity (and the burden) of trying to make things better.

Once you recognize that getting your way requires creating a winning coalition -- no matter if you are dealing with equals, with people who have more authority than you, or with people who have less authority than you -- then you have overcome a major obstacle to using the Prince System in pursuit of your goals. There still remain, however, several reasons why you might not use the system.

C. Thinking You Don't Have a Chance

Suppose you realize that getting your raise or changing the Little League schedule requires a winning coalition. If you are like most people, you are likely to interpret the slightest hint of rejection as evidence that you do not have a chance to win. It is sometimes easiest to accept rejection by assuming that a particular decision is out of your control, or in an extreme case, that all decisions are out of your

control -- in other words, the whole world is against you.
Such an assumption allows you to avoid accepting any responsibility for a lack of success. Blame can be placed elsewhere,
leaving you comfortable with your failures. Even in those
cases where, in reality, you do not have much of a chance,
thinking you have no chance will guarantee that your pessimis-
tic forecast comes true.

Automobiles would still be "unsafe at any speed" if Ralph
Nader had blamed his early failures on fate and conspiracy.
Nader spent ten years trying to get state legislatures and
Congress to enact laws reducing the safety hazards of auto-
mobiles. He had published a book, compiled massive amounts
of information, and devoted himself completely to the cause.
However, he had almost no success in challenging the automo-
bile industry and the legislators who were under its influence.

It would have been easy for Nader to view his lack of
success as a personal rejection based on conspiracy. Actually,
he had more reason than most of us to fall prey to such self-
defeating views. He had received threatening phone calls;
strange-looking characters were following him; and his friends
had been contacted and, under the pretext that he was being
considered for a job, they were asked if he was a homosexual.
As it turned out, some of these personal attacks were traced
back to General Motors, which ultimately apologized to him
personally.

Nader never accepted the proposition that he did not
have a chance. For him, a conspiracy (quite real) was just
a temporary winning coalition that had to be countered with
a coalition of his own. He stuck to his convictions and
built the organization and plans necessary to change the laws
governing auto safety in the United States.

You may have less ambitious and noble goals than Ralph
Nader, but you could easily underestimate your chances of
success. If you boss says "no" to a raise, a natural reaction
would be to kick the water cooler and then give up. You can
indulge yourself by deciding that the boss doesn't like you,
or that your horoscope was bad, that your biorhythms were
wrong, or maybe things will change, but that you have little
to do with it. All of these attitudes will allow you to
accept defeat gracefully, but they don't do much to improve
the quality of your life. You may do nothing, you may look
for another job where you would be more appreciated, you may
kick your dog, or you may complain to anyone who will listen,
but you would accept the decision without a fight.

To use the Prince System you must accept the responsibility that you could succeed. Whining or brooding may be more

gratifying in the short run, but it won't pay the bills.

D.   Thinking That You Can't Lose

A completely opposite attitude can also prevent you from
using the Prince System. You may think that because political
forces are so much on your side, a winning coalition is inevitable regardless of what you do or don't do. Obviously,
you do not take seriously Yogi Berra's brilliant insight,
"the game isn't over until it's over."

Two very different kinds of people make the erroneous
assumption that victory will be theirs: naive newcomers and
complacent autocrats. The former assume that since their
views are obviously right, everyone will see the light and
automatically line up on their side to form a winning coalition. Such people have no conception of the relativity of
their own beliefs and feel that reason and virtue will overcome any misguided opposition that may develop.

Naive newcomers are rarely found in formal political
situations. When people become involved in politics or governmental leadership, they generally lose most of the misplaced
faith in their own reason and virtue. Occasionally, in revolutionary situations such as the student protests against the
war in Vietnam or the fundamentalist revolution in Iran, some
of the rank and file may believe that right is on their side
and victory is inevitable. But in legislatures, city governments, and other formal systems, the naive do not last very
long.

However, in less formal situations such as the politics
of zoning and parent-teacher's associations, you will find
people who think making speeches is enough to win. They believe that once people see the problem in the "right" perspec-
tive their position will be supported. It is interesting to
watch such people because they will either keep talking,
ignoring the fact that no one is listening, or, if they realize that they are getting nowhere, they become as enraged as
some of the 1960s' students, or drop out embittered and alienated by the experience.

Complacent autocrats also suffer from a false sense of
security. After years of getting their way, they forget that
their success depended on a winning coalition. They may have
used force as Hitler did to maintain order, but even his ability to use that force depended on support from the military
establishment. They may have obtained power through an over-
whelming electoral mandate or a process that everyone at the

time considered to be highly legitimate, but their ability to lead also depended on the willingness of others to follow on a continuing basis. To believe in the permanence of your own authority is as preposterous as to believe in your own immortality.

Complacent autocrats can be found in the home, on the job, in the church -- in every organization. They may have at one time approached the task of building a consensus with vigor and openness, or they may possess what psychologists call an authoritarian personality. They may have ignored the views and feelings of others for some period of time, and they may continue to do so indefinitely. But once those who suffer under their rule see a chance to challenge their authority, they will act with vengeance, and the authority will disappear as fast as you can say, "L'etat c'est moi." In large-scale political situations such as the downfall of the monarchy in revolutionary France and the Shah of Iran, as well as everyday situations like the challenging of a father by his son, the process is always disruptive and frequently destructive.

To succeed and sustain yourself in politics you have to run scared and continuously work to build support for yourself and your goals. You have to recognize the need for a winning coalition and the possibility of losing that coalition at any time. When you have this attitude, you are ready to start using the Prince System.

E. Personality Is Enough

Another reason why you may ignore the need to build winning coalitions to get your way is that you think personality and personal contact is enough. How many times in your life have you thought that if you could only have a few extra minutes with a prospective employer, an admission officer, or a key buyer, you would succeed? True, personal contact is very important. (This is why many key decision-makers shield themselves from those who want something from them.) But it is a mistake to think that personal contact is sufficient.

Salesmen are particularly prone to this weakness. They associate a sale with an affirmation of their own personal worth: "The customer buys because he likes me. Sure my product is good and my price is competitive, but the only thing that differentiates it from my competitors is me." In part, this view is required as a necessary antidote to the repeated rejections which are a necessary part of even the most successful salesman's career. In part, this view results from the salesman's face-to-face linkage between his company and the individual customer. The personal touch is essential and so personality has come to be seen as the determinant of success.

However, effective salesmen find that many sales depend on the decisions of several people within a company. In addition to the direct buyer, the people who participate directly or indirectly in the decision may be the company's purchasing agent, the buyer's boss, and the people who will have to use the product. When it comes to big ticket items like computers or production equipment, people outside the buyer's company may become involved. The bank, an outside consultant, and even the salesman's own credit manager may eventually have a role in the decision to buy. In this kind of situation, a good personality helps, but a carefully planned strategy to build a winning coalition is essential.

Others also fall prey to the myth that personality is everything. Even though you may have a solid personal relationship with your boss, if your ideas threaten others who also have a good relationship you will quickly find yourself out in the cold. Politicians, who should know better, often emphasize the importance of personality. This tendency can be seen in the inordinate amount of money politicians spend to convey an appealing public image. Research is beginning to show that candidates' positions on issues, and whether times are good or bad, are often more important than the personal appeal of the candidate.

It may serve your ego to believe that you achieve your goals in life because you are so lovable, but you will be much more successful if you realize when it's necessary to build a winning coalition in order to succeed. This fact goes a long way toward explaining why so many successful politicians, businessmen, and organization leaders succeed despite their distasteful personalities.

F. Politics Is Bad

You may consciously ignore the need to build a winning coalition because you think the practice of politics is beneath you. Our culture doesn't place a very high value on politicians. Just read the entries under "Politics" in Bartlett's Familiar Quotations should you have any doubts. These range from Thesmophoriazusae (410 B.C.): "Under every stone lurks a politician" through Shakespeare: "A politician ...one that would circumvent God," to Will Rogers who observed that "all politics is applesauce" and further that "more men have been elected between sundown and sunup than ever were elected between sunup and sundown." Most of us suspect that real people, or at least decent people, don't play politics.

It is not hard to understand why politics and politicians have such a bad name. First, because of our highly sophisti- cated and secular education, we can no longer blame the world's ills on fate, the gods, or lack of scientific knowledge. Poli- ticians are the best culprits to blame for hunger, war, disease, and taxes. Second, politics -- the pursuit of a winning coali- tion -- frequently requires compromise and flexibility which is felt to be inconsistent with freedom and individuality. It is a sign of weakness and lack of commitment. That is why "politics make strange bedfellows" and politicians parti- cipate in "pork barrel" legislation. Most people don't want to be the former or eat out of the latter. Third, newscasts, newspapers, television magazine programs like "60 Minutes," and weekly news magazines enjoy slinging mud at politicians in order to increase their audience. Consequently, even the most well-informed and critical leader is likely to come around to the view of H.L. Mencken who made part of his repu- tation by mercilessly attacking politicians, making among many other vicious statements: "A government, at bottom, is nothing more than a gang of men, and as a practical matter most of them are inferior men." (Minority Report, p. 57.) Finally, people overcome by a winning coalition find it comforting to vent their frustration and prepare the groundwork for a future victory by blaming the wrong and "obviously irrational" deci- sion on politics.

The negative attitudes toward public politics also in- fluence ideas people have about how to get things done in their home, office, or school. Nobody likes to be accused of playing "office politics." Such activities are frequently viewed with as much disdain as giving trade secrets to your competitor. The wife who tries to build a winning coalition to get father to agree to a family vacation may be risking a major crisis over her relationship with the husband. As a result of these attitudes, politics played outside the formal arena is usually done quietly, which in the long run further contributes to its negative image.

In order to succeed in many of life's endeavors, however, it is necessary to come to grips with the question of the good- ness of politics. Not all politics is good. It depends on the ends pursued and the means used to achieve a winning coali- tion. Hitler was bad on both accounts. But, the heart of politics -- getting more people to support you than oppose you on a chosen issue -- is as noble as any activity. It acknowledges your willingness to share your feelings and ad- just your needs to others. It is part of the human condition which you can choose to avoid only at considerable cost. If you do, you should avoid it because you have made a conscious decision that you do not want to play the game rather than an unconscious decision caused by the inherent bias in our culture toward playing politics.

Politics is like talking, smiling, writing, or any other act of communication. It can be done for noble or ignoble purposes. It is important not to confuse the goals with the means used to achieve them. One such goal, we must admit, for some of the people some of the time, is politics as an end in itself. Some people do like to use politics to manipulate people just for the fun of it. We don't like this any more than you do. But the existence of liars doesn't lead us to conclude that talking is bad, and the existence of flirts doesn't lead us to ban smiling. So the existence of people on power trips shouldn't lead us to avoid or reject politics.

G.   When You Should Use the Prince System

The Prince System is designed to be used by people who see the need to build a winning coalition in order to get their way in a specific situation. We have just explained why people prefer not to think about their problems in this way. If you can avoid the attitudes just described, and you see the need to build a winning coalition, you are ready to use the Prince System.

The system is an aid to those who need to have a winning coalition in order to get their way. Some people have a natural ability to play politics and, for them, the Prince System is merely a formalization of the way they think and act. It is a formalization, we might add, that will improve their natural political effectiveness. But for most of us who are not used to thinking this way, the Prince System may represent a revolution in the way you conduct your personal, business, and public relationships. As a tool for building winning coalitions, it can be used or misused. The remainder of this package will tell you how to do the former and avoid the latter.

You should use the Prince System in the following types of situations:

1.   Where you have a specific objective in which decisions by several people will determine your success.

2.   Where decisions lead to a specific event or set of events. An objective to make your teenagers more responsible is inappropriate, but an objective to make your teenager

save $10 a week for college is appropriate. In other
words, your objective must be sufficiently concrete so
that it is clear when you have succeeded or when you
have not. Objectives that have to do with persuading
people, governments, or organizations to change their
general attitudes or overall behavior cannot be achieved
using the system, although using the system may have a
long-run effect in the desired direction.

3.   Where you feel your objective is sufficiently important
      to you that building a winning coalition formally and
      applying the system are worth the effort. We have al-
      ready talked about how time-consuming and costly it is
      to build a winning coalition. The Prince System can be
      applied quickly and easily, but it does take additional
      time and effort. So, it is a tool that you apply for-
      mally only in important situations. Once you learn the
      system, however, you will be able to apply it informally,
      with little additional effort.

      The balance of the learning package tells you how to
apply the Prince System once you have decided on a specific
objective. Before you read any further, it is best to come
up with an objective that you would like to achieve but which
is opposed by one or more people. Be certain that you state
the objective in the form of a specific event such as to obtain a raise, buy a new car, lower your property taxes, or
win the presidency of a local organization. The objective
should also be important to you.

CHAPTER 2: STEPS IN COMPLETING THE PRINCE SYSTEM TO PROVIDE A POLITICAL FORECAST

The Prince Political Accounting System is a technique for assessing the impact of various individuals, groups, and organizations on public policy decisions. The basic assumption behind the Prince System is that in order to assess the impact of relevant individuals, groups, and organizations on any decision, it is necessary to do the following:

- Identify the individuals, groups, and organizations (the "actors") that are likely to have a direct or indirect impact on the decision. This includes those that have a formal role in the making or blocking of the decision. It also means including those who have an indirect impact -- those making it either easier or harder to carry out a decision after it is made.

- Determining whether each actor supports, opposes, or is neutral toward the decision. (This is called "issue position.")

- Determine how effective each actor is in blocking the decision, helping make it happen, or effecting the implementation of a decision. (This is called "power.")

- Determine how important the decision is to each actor. (This is called "salience.")

When making decisions, key individuals -- the president, a legislator, a regional governmental official, a business executive, a school superintendent, or the head of the household -- always perform these kinds of analyses, if only informally. The purpose of the Prince System is to provide a systematic framework and checklist which decision-makers can use to make sure they carry out the kind of analysis required to assess the consequences of a decision. The Prince System also aids decision-makers in organizing their staffs and making use of knowledgeable observers.

The basic steps followed in completing the Prince System are shown below:

A. Define the Issue

An issue is a proposed decision or action which is likely
to generate controversy. It may be a local ordinance, a
national policy decision, or an international foreign policy
issue. The Prince System can be applied when the proposed
decision is clearly defined in specific terms, in a phrase
beginning with a verb. If an issue is defined as "protecting
the environment" or "improving the efficiency of an agency's
regulatory procedure," it would not be possible to complete a
Prince Analysis. But the analysis can be done on specific
issues such as "issue a general regulation controlling the
landfill activities of private landowners." The key is found
in the verb used to phrase the decision. Verbs such as "protect" or "improve" are undesirable because they do not adequately specify the required action. Verbs like "restrict,"
"vote," "oppose," "permit," or "build" are much more useful.

While decisions or actions need to be specifically defined
in order to conduct analysis, trying to guess at the exact
detail of the final formulation is not required. One of the
main characteristics of reaching decisions affecting many
actors is that the action is frequently redefined and modified
as a result of the process of reaching a decision. The decision may begin as "issue a general regulation that governs
landfill activities of private landowners," and become modified
to "issue a general regulation that governs landfill activities
of private landowners and commercial property under a certain
acreage." Such a change may be required to obtain the support
of important groups to solve technical problems in administering
the permit. The Prince System can be applied to any number of
proposed decisions (including redefinitions and modifications)
as long as it is clear what specific action is involved at each
point along the way.

Another important consideration in picking a decision is
to make sure that there is both significant support and opposition. It is pointless to analyze a decision that is either so
well accepted or so widely opposed that the outcome is obvious.
Of course, few decisions affecting the public result in over-
whelming support or opposition. However, when they do come
along they do not need to be analyzed systematically.

B. Identify Actors

An actor is any individual, group, or organization that
ought to be considered in making the decision or in carrying
it out after it has been made. Reasons for including an actor

are any of the following: the actor has substantial legal
authority; the actor has political influence to promote or
obstruct the decision; or the actor will be seriously affected
by the decision and may either help or hinder its implementation, even though it may not have much of a say in the actual
making of the decision.

Identifying the actors to be considered is one of the most
important steps in the Prince System. Omitting an important
actor or incorrectly grouping actors can distort the analysis
so much that the analysis becomes useless.

In order to keep the analysis within feasible bounds,
limit the number of actors to twenty -- or even less, if possible. In situations where time is short, try to limit the
number of actors to ten or less. The reason for limiting the
number of actors is to limit the time required for listing and
calculations required for the Prince System.

The principal way to limit the number of actors is to
group individuals and organizations into collective actors for
the purpose of analysis. The process of grouping frequently
appears arbitrary and, as mentioned earlier, can seriously
bias your results if it is not done carefully. However, there
are some guidelines that will assist you in grouping actors to
help improve the accuracy of your analysis:

- Group actors together that have the same economic
  interests. In dealing with an environmental issue,
  for example, all private developers might be grouped
  together for this reason.

- Do not group together actors that have veto power.
  This especially holds for governmental actors. For
  example, the U.S. Fish and Wildlife Service might
  be kept separate from the Environmental Protection
  Agency, but similar state agencies for natural
  resources and environmental regulation could be
  combined.

- Do not group together actors if there is disagreement
  among them or if their components have widely unequal
  power. For example, a city government could be combined as a single actor if there were general agreement among all members of the government concerning
  the issue and if each person in the governing unit
  had approximately equal power. If there were disagreements, or if some members were much more powerful
  than others, it would be preferable to divide them
  into two (or more) actors.

- Select a configuration of actors that taken together
  constitute a reasonable picture of the overall power
  distribution. Do not include an excess of actors
  that gives one side an unrealistic weighting. If
  there is one collective actor with an immense amount
  of power, that actor should be divided into enough
  smaller actors so that the total power configuration
  is accurately reflected.

These guidelines are admittedly quite general. The designation
of the actors in the Prince System is at least as much an art
as a science. Your judgment in conducting the analysis is
vital at every step. In one sense, this might be viewed as a
weakness in the technique, but not really. The system is a
way of organizing and guiding judgment, not eliminating it.
It would be foolish to ignore the importance of judgment and
balanced insight (even if it were possible to do so) in the
selection of actors as well as in the other aspects of Prince
analysis.

C.   Estimate Issue Position, Power, and Salience for Each
     Actor (See Table 1)

Issue Position is the current general attitude of the
actor toward the decision. It is expressed as a number ranging
from +3 to -3 to indicate whether or not the actor supports
(+3, +2, or +1); is neutral toward (0); or opposes (-1, -2, or
-3) the decision. A "+3" is assigned if the actor is firmly
in favor of the issue and is unlikely to change; "+2" or "+1"
indicates reduced levels of firmness of the actor's support.
Similarly, a "-3" indicates firm opposition while a "-2" or
"-1" indicates there is some softness in the opposition.

Power is defined as the degree to which the actor can
exert influence, directly or indirectly, in support of or in
opposition to the decision, relative to all other actors. The
basis of an actor's power as well as the ways in which this
power may be exercised are varied. Power may be based on such
factors as group size, wealth, physical resources, institu-
tional authority, prestige, and political skill. Power is
expressed as a number ranging from 1 to 3. A "1" is assigned
if the actor has a slight amount of power; a "2" if the actor
has moderate power. A "3" is assigned if an actor has substantial influence, especially if the actor can veto or prevent
the implementation of the decision.

Salience is defined as the importance the actor attaches
to supporting or opposing the decision relative to all other

TABLE 1: PRINCE CHART

ISSUE: _____

(State in terms of a desired political outcome, using a phrase beginning with a verb.)

ACTORS	ISSUE POSITION	X	POWER	X	SALIENCE	=	TOTAL SUPPORT BY ACTOR
	-3-0-+3		1-3		1-3		
		X		X		=	
		X		X		=	
		X		X		=	
		X		X		=	
		X		X		=	
		X		X		=	
		X		X		=	
		X		X		=	

Totals: A - Scores of all actors supporting the issue: __
B - Absolute value of actors opposing the issue: __
C - Scores of actors with zero issue positions: __
D - Totals A, B, C: __
E - Total A + 1/2 of Total C: __
Probability of Support = $\dfrac{E}{D}$ = _____

decisions with which that actor is concerned. Salience is expressed as a number ranging from 1 to 3. A "1" indicates slight interest or concern for the issue regardless of the issue position or power. A "2" is assigned for those actors that have moderate concern. A "3" is reserved for those actors that assign the highest priority to the issue.

The task of estimating each actor's issue position, power, and salience can be facilitated by the following suggestions.

When estimating an actor's <u>issue position</u>:

- Read and listen to what the actor says about the issue.

- Deduce from the actor's economic, social, or political standing what its position is likely to be on the basis of self-interest.

- Weigh the implications of concrete interests against what it has said. When in doubt, use concrete interests for your estimate over mere verbalizations.

- Look for differences among individuals and factions within a collective actor. Look for inconsistencies in statements by an individual actor. If the contrasting positions seem evenly balanced, assign a "0" (neutral) issue position. If there seems a slight positive or negative balance toward the issue, assign a "+1" or "-1" for the actor's issue position.

When estimating an actor's <u>power</u>:

- Ask if the actor has the resources either to block a decision or to make one occur.

- Determine if legal authority is a consideration and if the actor possesses a large share of the authority.

- Consider whether an actor has the ability to help or hinder the carrying out of a decision. (This is why constituency groups have power.)

- Determine, if wealth is a consideration, how much wealth the actor has.

- Do not assume that an actor powerful on one set of issues is necessarily powerful on all issues. It is true that an actor's high power on one issue means it <u>may</u> have power on other issues, but it does not assure high power across the board.

- Consider the allies and enemies of the actor. Powerful allies makes the actor powerful; powerful enemies diminish the actor's power.

When estimating salience:

- Determine the frequency and intensity with which the actor makes public statements about the decision.

- Deduce from the actor's social, political, and economic interests the importance it is likely to attach to the decision.

- Watch out for the fact that salience can be rapidly and substantially altered by external events and the intrusion of other issues.

- Remember that other decisions and factors compete for the actor's attention and, hence, its salience.

As with selecting actors, the assignment of issue position, power, and salience is something of an art. Systematic research can play an important role, but the importance of the skillful assessment of existing conditions by knowledgeable and sensible observers is absolutely essential. Therefore, it is important that those completing the charts be thoroughly familiar with the situation. They should talk to other knowledgeable people and gather all available information on the reactions of individuals, groups, and organizations to the proposed decision.

D. Calculate the Weights for Each Actor and for the Whole System

After the estimates are made for each actor, the next step is to calculate the weights each actor contributes in the decision. This is done by multiplying issue position times power times salience for each actor. Issue position (alone of the three variables) may be either positive or negative. (The other two are always positive.) Therefore, the sign of the issue position will be the sign of the weight for each actor. After each actor's weight is calculated, determine the overall sum by adding the signed numbers.

The information you gather is summarized below in Table 2. Notice that issue position can have either positive numbers (if the actor in question favors a decision), negative numbers (if the actor opposes a decision), or zero (if the actor is

neutral). Power and salience range from 1 to 3 -- with no
negative values. And friendship-neutrality-hostility is
indicated by a plus, a zero, or a negative sign.

TABLE 2: RANGE OF VARIABLES USED IN THE PRINCE POLITICAL
ACCOUNTING SYSTEM AND VERBAL INTERPRETATION OF
EACH VARIABLE.

Issue Position	Power	Salience
+3 Strong support	+3 Strong power	+3 High salience
+2 Moderate support	+2 Moderate power	+2 Moderate salience
+1 Weak support	+1 Weak power	+1 Weak salience
0 Neutrality		
-1 Weak opposition		
-2 Moderate opposition		
-3 Strong opposition		

E.   Calculating Probabilities

By completing the following steps, the weights calculated
for each actor can also be used to estimate the probability of
the decision's being adopted.

1. Add together the scores of all the actors supporting the
    decision. Call this total "A."

2. Add together the scores of all the actors opposing the
    issue. Eliminate the minus sign. (This is called taking
    the "absolute value" of the number.) Call this total "B."

3. Multiply the non-zero scores of all the actors that have
    a neutral issue position, and add together these scores.
    Call this total "C."

4. Add together "A," "B," and "C." This is the total of all
    the power weights in the particular system as you have
    described it with your Prince analysis. Call this total
    "D."

5. Add together "A" and <u>one-half</u> the value of "C," the neutral actors' scores. Call this total "E." The reason for including one-half the value of "C" is that the neutral actors are equally likely, in the future, to be either supporters or opponents of the issue. The best way to represent this 50-50 situation in the absence of other information is to include just half of the neutral actors' scores with the positive weights. Total "E" is the sum of the best estimate of the likely weights to be exerted in support of the issue.

6. Divide "E" (the weights supporting the issue) by "D" (the total weights in the system.) The resulting fraction is proportion of positive weights in relation to the total weights. It can be interpreted as the likelihood that the issue will be supported -- that the decision, law, or whatever is represented by the issue, will be implemented. This fraction, like all probability numbers, ranges from 0.0 (no chance of occurrence) to 1.00 (certainty of occurrence). These numbers are frequently reported as 0% to 100%. Note that if the probability is low, this may mean two things: either the decision will be defeated, or it will continue as a controversial issue without being decided one way or another. The closer the supporting and opposing weights are to each other, the more likely the issue will continue as a controversial topic without being resolved one way or another.

Table 3 on the next page has a completed Prince chart on the issue of maintaining present tuition rates for the next academic year at a university.

TABLE 3: PRINCE CHART

ISSUE: <u>Maintain the Same Tuition Cost from 1980-81 to 1981-82</u>
(State in terms of a desired political outcome, using a phrase beginning with a verb.)

ACTORS	ISSUE POSITION	X	POWER	X	SALIENCE	=	TOTAL SUPPORT BY ACTOR
	-3-0-+3		1-3		1-3		
Administration	-2	X	3	X	3	=	-18
Board of Trustees	0	X	2	X	2	=	(4)
SA/Students in Senate	+3	X	1	X	2	=	+ 6
Faculty in Senate	-2	X	3	X	2	=	-12
Parents Office	+2	X	2	X	1	=	+ 4
Budget Committee	-2	X	1	X	3	=	- 6

Totals: A - Scores of all actors supporting the issue: <u>10</u>
B - Absolute value of actors opposing the issue: <u>36</u>
C - Scores of actors with zero issue positions: <u>4</u>
D - Totals A, B, C: <u>50</u>
E - Total A + 1/2 of Total C: <u>12</u>
Probability of Support = $\frac{E}{D}$ = $\frac{12}{50}$ = .24 (24%)

Note that the students and the representatives of the parents are in favor of maintaining the present levels. They have a weight of 10; this is total "A." The administration, the general faculty, and the faculty senate budget committee are opposed. Their scores, total "B," have an absolute value of 36. The board of trustees is neutral; their score, total "C," is 4. The total scores of all the actors (counting the product of the non-zero scores for the board of trustees) is 50. The total of these in favor of holding the line on tuition is 10; to this is added 2 points (one-half of the score of the neutral board of trustees) for a total of 12, total "E." The basic Prince calculation then is "E" divided by "D," 12/50, or only .24 -- also expressed as a 24% chance that the present tuition rate will remain the same for the forthcoming academic year. In other words, this forecast indicates the chances are quite small that the rates will remain the same.

You should note that this analysis could have been prepared by having the issue stated: "Raise tuition rates for the forth-coming year." In this case, the signs of the issue positions would be reversed. The resulting calculations would have been based on a total of 36 points for those supporting an increase, plus 2 points for the neutral board of trustees, for a total of 38 divided by 50 -- or a probability of 76% that the increase would take place. Saying that there is only a 24% chance that no increase will occur is the same as saying that there is a 76% chance that an increase will occur. (Incidently, the increase did occur, confirming the unhappy prediction.) It is a matter of convenience whether the issue is stated affirma-tively (making an action occur) or negatively (preventing an action from occurring).

26

EXERCISE 1: Conducting a Prince Analysis

Identify a public policy -- either one existing or one proposed -- and conduct a Prince analysis to determine whether
or not the Policy will continue (if it already exists) or will
be implemented (if it is proposed). Complete each of the first
five steps outlined in this chapter on the Prince chart below.

ISSUE: _____

(State in terms of a desired political outcome, using a phrase
beginning with a verb.)

ACTORS	ISSUE POSITION -3-0-+3	X	POWER 1-3	X	SALIENCE 1-3	=	TOTAL SUPPORT BY ACTOR
		X		X		=	
		X		X		=	
		X		X		=	
		X		X		=	
		X		X		=	
		X		X		=	
		X		X		=	
		X		X		=	

Totals: A - Scores of all actors supporting the issue: ___
         B - Absolute value of actors opposing the issue: ___
         C - Scores of actors with zero issue positions: ___
         D - Totals A, B, C: ___
         E - Total A + 1/2 of Total C: ___
         Probability of Support = $\dfrac{E}{D}$ = _____

CHAPTER 3: FORMULATING STRATEGIES

One of the prime values of the Prince Political Accounting System is that it enables you to formulate on a systematic basis strategies that you might want to pursue to achieve a political outcome. In order to use the system, the first thing that you must decide is what political outcome you would like to achieve. In terms of the probability estimate generated by your analysis, do you want a higher or lower probability? Once you have decided that question, you need to take the role of one of the actors in the Prince chart or to take a role that you can visualize would allow you to influence actors in the Prince chart.

The Prince chart gives you a kind of political "snapshot" of what is going to happen in the near future. In order to make longer run forecasts, and, most importantly, in order to decide on a strategy to help make things change the way you would like them to, you need two other Prince tools -- a Friendship-Neutrality-Hostility chart and a Prince Political Map. Once you have mastered these tools, you will be able to formulate political strategies.

A.   Friendship-Neutrality-Hostility Chart

The Friendship-Neutrality-Hostility chart is a table in which each actor is related to each other with a "+" to denote political friendship, a "0" to denote neutrality, and a "-" to denote political hostility. The three signs can be used to predict whether or not the actor in the row will attempt to agree with, remain neutral toward, or disagree with the actor designated by the column on any given issue the two are likely to become concerned with. (The "X" refers to how each actor feels about itself. Since this is a political and not a psychoanalytical approach, no scores are provided.)

A sample chart is shown on the next page in Table 4, using the actors on the tuition issue discussed earlier.

TABLE 4:   FRIENDSHIP-NEUTRALITY-HOSTILITY CHART

This Actor feels about this Actor:

	Administration	Board of Trustees	Students	Faculty	Parents Office	Budget Committee
Administration	X	+	+	+	-	+
Board of Trustees	+	X	+	+	0	-
Students	-	-	X	-	+	-
Faculty	-	-	-	X	+	-
Parents Office	-	+	+	+	X	-
Budget Committee	+	+	-	0	0	X

The Friendship-Neutrality-Hostility chart can help you pre-dict which actors are more likely to agree or disagree with each other over the long haul by looking down the column of that actor. For example, looking down the administration's column, we would expect that the administration could get the board of trustees or the budget committee to back it easier than the students, faculty, or the parents office. These patterns are relatively stable and therefore can be used to gauge the degree to which changes in issue position might occur.

B.   Prince Political Map

The second major tool for deciding on strategies is to use the information in the Prince charts to construct a Prince Political Map which is a kind of political map of the issue. To construct a map, each actor is placed along the vertical axis according to whether it supports, is neutral toward, or opposed to the action, and by the certainty of the actors' issue positions. Actors are located along the horizontal axis according to the score they have when their power and salience is multiplied together.

Actors located in the upper right corner of the chart are those that exert the maximum weight in support of the action. Actors in the lower right corner of the chart are those that exert the maximum weight against the action. Actors located in the upper left are strong supporters of the action, but carry little weight in determining its outcome. Actors in the lower left are opponents with little influence.

On the next page in Table 5 is a political map based on the Prince chart in Table 3.

Notice that the actors opposed to the tuition increase are in the upper left corner, indicating their weakness in trying to keep tuition costs down.

The map also shows the key role of the board of trustees. Clearly, someone who either supports or opposes the tuition increase should work to convince the board.

While each map is unique in many respects, certain general patterns frequently appear. Tables 6-9 contain examples of typical patterns. Note that in three of the four illustrative charts (charts B-D), the probability of the action's occurrence is low. However, each of these three charts presents patterns of actor distributions that indicate quite different interpretations of the forecasts about the outcome. A summary analysis is provided with each of the four charts.

TABLE 5:   PRINCE POLITICAL MAP

ISSUE: <u>Maintain the Same Tuition Cost from 1980-1981 to 1981-1982</u>

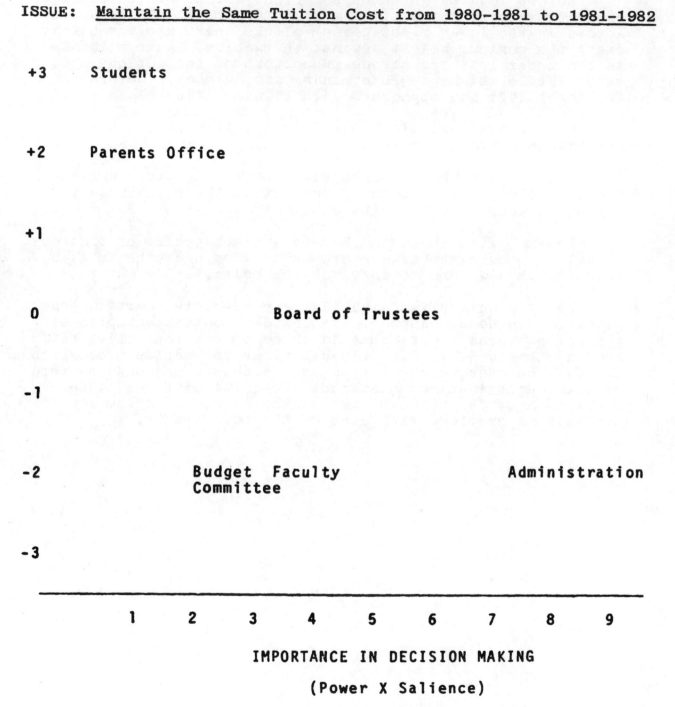

IMPORTANCE IN DECISION MAKING

(Power X Salience)

TABLE 6:   CHART A -- SUBSTANTIAL SUPPORT

Most of the actors are in the upper right-hand corner, indicating that the over-
whelming weight is in favor of the outcome. A few actors are opposed; however, they
possess much less weight in determining the outcome. Even if the opponents become
more strongly opposed, they will not significantly change the likelihood of the
outcome's occurrence.

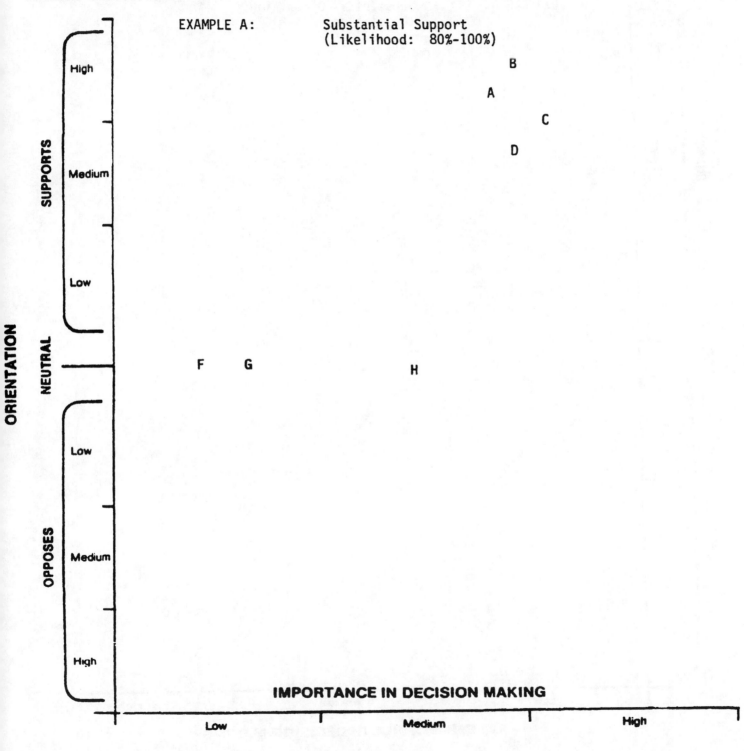

EXAMPLE A: Substantial Support
                    (Likelihood: 80%-100%)

TABLE 7:   CHART B -- SUBSTANTIAL OPPOSITION

Most of the actors are in the lower right-hand corner, indicating that the over-whelming weight is in opposition to the outcome. Even if those who are moderate in their opposition change to support, the net weight of the players will still be against the outcome's occurrence.

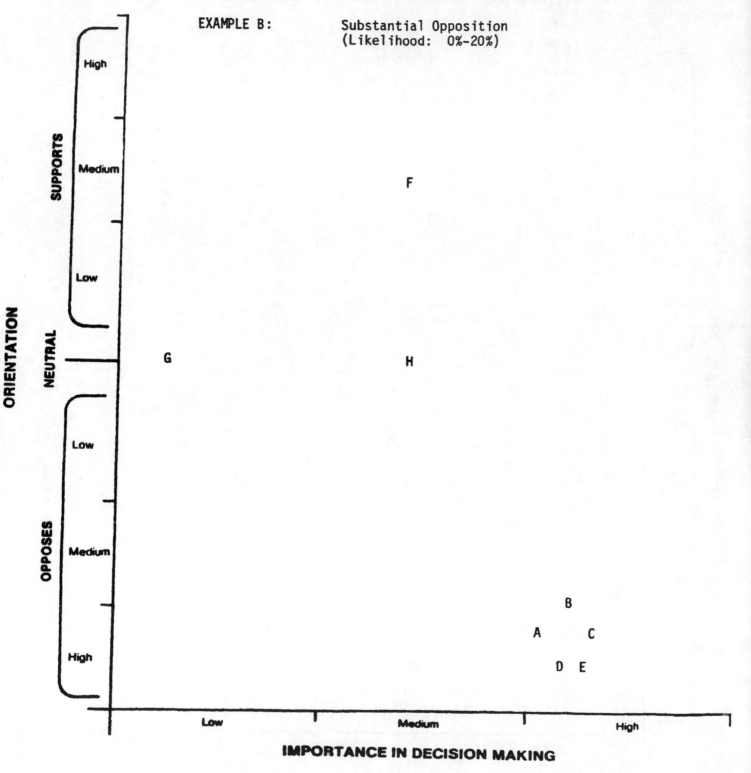

EXAMPLE B: Substantial Opposition
(Likelihood: 0%-20%)

TABLE 8: CHART C -- SHARP POLARIZATION

The number and weight of the players is about evenly split between the supporters and the opponents of the outcome. The forecast in this case is that: 1) no decision will be made soon; and 2) controversy over the outcome will be high and will contribute to conflict.

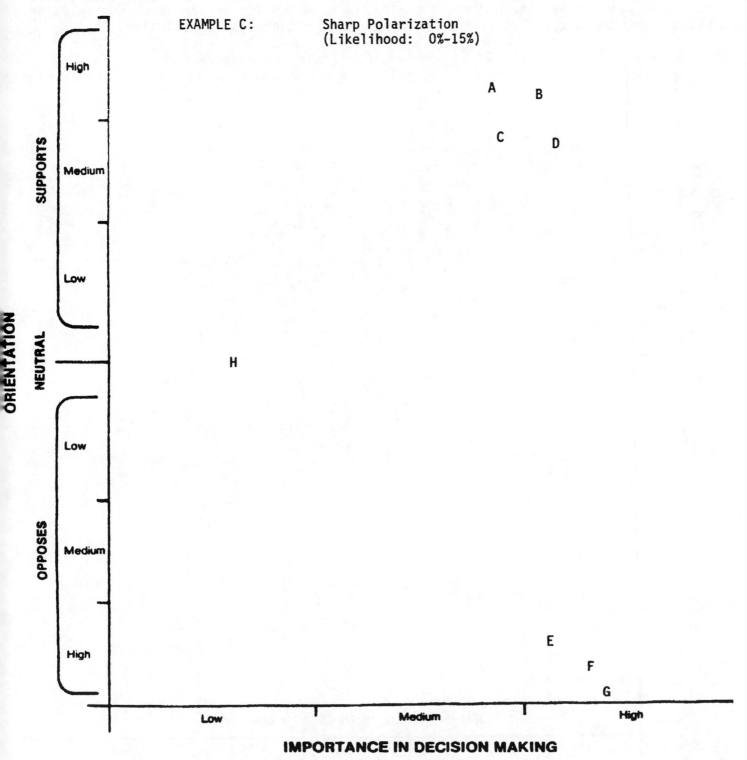

EXAMPLE C: Sharp Polarization
(Likelihood: 0%-15%)

TABLE 9: CHART D -- UNSETTLED SITUATION

A few actors strongly support the outcome and a few strongly oppose it, but the bulk of the actors are either undecided or lacking in decisive weight in determining the outcome. This is the situation in which forecasting is most difficult. The only certainty is that a positive decision will not be made soon. However, more information will have to be obtained about the impact of other issues and about the relationships among the actors before the outcome can be more precisely estimated.

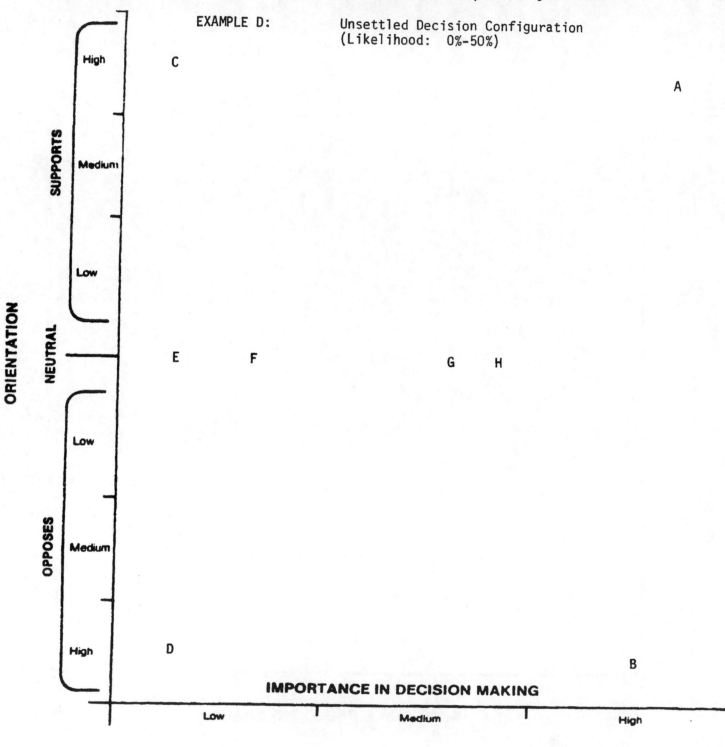

EXAMPLE D: Unsettled Decision Configuration
(Likelihood: 0%-50%)

C.   Strategy Guidelines

After making a decision on what your political goal is and whom you will represent, you can explore strategies under the following principles:

1.   Formulate your decision so that you get the most important components of what you want, while making potential opposition actors as happy as possible.

2.   Try to stimulate actors who are not on the Prince chart to become interested or powerful enough to warrant placing them on the Prince chart.

3.   Change issue position of actors so that they agree with you, or if they already agree with you, more firmly agree with you. This can be done by:

   a) Using arguments of a symbolic or factual kind
   b) Making promises
   c) Making threats
   d) Use the Friendship-Neutrality-Hostility chart to identify friends who are most likely to agree with you, and enemies who are least likely to agree with you.

4.   Change power of yourself and those who support you relative to those who do not support your position by:

   a) Gaining wealth
   b) Improving your organization to deliver votes, money, or other expressions of support (e.g., letters to congressmen)
   c) Acquiring knowledge and expertise
   d) Making friends
   e) Isolating enemies

5.   Change salience of yourself and those who support you relative to those who do not support your position by:

   a) Raising salience:

      i) create an event that generates publicity

      ii) distribute information about the issue

   b) Lowering salience:

      i) keep issue out of the press or other publicity media

      ii) raise another issue that deflects attention of actors whose salience you wish to lower

        iii) the number of issues an actor can have high
            salience on is limited; introducing a new high
            salience issue may reduce the salience on other
            issues

6. In general:

    a) Always remember to consider salience when making a
       compromise. It is frequently prudent to offer a
       little extra to the side with the higher salience
    b) The poorer the actor, the higher the salience on
       growth issues
    c) As long as resources increase, political support
       can be maintained by adopting public policies that
       satisfy the most salient interest of each actor
    d) Bureaucrats use jargon and committees for the poli-
       tical purpose of keeping salience low
    e) Bureaucrats have little power over broad public policy
       questions; but they often have tremendous power vis-
       vis limited decisions that can be very important to
       individuals. Therefore, don't ignore them in your
       calculations
    f) The degree to which power is centralized or decentra-
       lized among the political actors should shape your
       political strategies

EXERCISE 2: Using Strategies

Choose the role of one of the actors from the Prince chart
completed in Exercise 1 and develop two strategies to raise
the probability of your desired outcome. Use the Prince
Political Map and Friendship-Neutrality-Hostility chart to
plan your strategy and to indicate what change you think it
is reasonable to accomplish.

PRINCE POLITICAL MAP

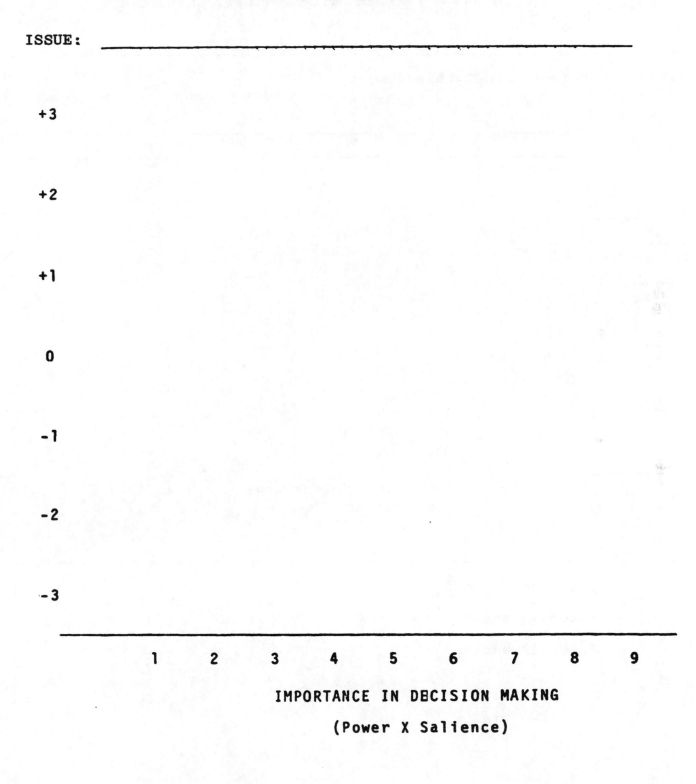

ISSUE: _____

ISSUE POSITION

+3

+2

+1

0

-1

-2

-3

1   2   3   4   5   6   7   8   9

IMPORTANCE IN DECISION MAKING

(Power X Salience)

FRIENDSHIP-NEUTRALITY-HOSTILITY CHART

This Actor feels about this Actor:

_____   _____   _____   _____   _____   _____

_____

_____

_____

_____

_____

_____

Key: + Actor is friendly

  - Actor is enemy

  0 Actor is neutral

CHAPTER 4:   HOW TO OBTAIN DATA FOR YOUR OWN PRINCE ANALYSIS

One of the most difficult tasks you must face in using the Prince Political Accounting System is to come up with the numbers for the charts. The point to remember is this: You are making estimates of how people relate to you and to each other. Numbers used in research and problem-solving by everybody -- physicists, economists, generals -- are also estimates. You will naturally want to make your estimates as carefully as possible. In the preceding chapters, we hope we have given you some suggestions for making better estimates. But if you feel that what you are putting down on paper is only an approximation of what the world is "really" like -- congratulations! You are in the very good company of scientists and scholars who deep in their hearts feel the same way, but who are rarely called upon to admit it openly. In a more positive sense, you are in good company as well because, like the scientist, what you lose in detail about each feeling of each element you consider, you will more than likely gain in usable knowledge about overall patterns and possibilities in the world around you.

There are, as a matter of fact, lots of social science techniques for transforming people's feelings and capabilities into numbers that can be used in the Prince charts. If you have access to opinion polls or other systematically gathered information, you should really be able to swing Prince. But we are not going to assume that you are always in such a happy condition. Even Dr. Gallup himself is liable to be caught in situations where he has to make spur-of-the-moment applications of Prince.

This chapter presents two ways of collecting information for Prince charts. First, we will discuss informal methods where you have neither the time nor the opportunity to use research tools. Second, we will discuss ways you can derive information from written materials. Each approach has its strengths and limitations, but a knowledge of both will go a long way toward answering the data question.

A.   Some Informal Methods of Collecting Information

Obviously, there are some general guidelines you can follow when filling in each of the charts. For the issue posi- tions of the actors, read and listen to what they have said about the issue. Of course, you cannot take what they have said at face value, so check what they say for consistency and always take into account the audience to whom they are talking. Even here the chart will help you because you can assume that, when one political actor is talking to another, his or her issue position will appear closer to the target of his/her remarks than it really is. Use your common sense in figuring out where people stand and you will probably not miss very much.

For the power of political actors on issues, you need only ask yourself the question, "Who has the resources to stop an event from taking place or to make an event occur?" Mother may control the purse-strings, but father manages the budget. That is why those two in our example have so much power over the money issues. In more complicated political settings, power is much more diffused. Congress controls the purse-strings, but the executive branch has the capacity to act. In fact, it is precisely because power is generally diffused that the essence of politics is collective action. If one person could do anything he or she wanted, there would be no need for a political accounting system.

For the salience of the issue for each political actor, the task is not very difficult. The frequency with which an actor talks about the subject is a clear indication of his or her interest in it. We can also assume that the more things somebody wants, the less intense he feels about any one of them. Measurement gets a little complicated when we start talking about groups. In a group -- whether it be the Kiwanis Club or the Democratic party -- the leadership acts for the group. However, the salience the leadership feels for parti- cular issues is directly related to the actual or anticipated awareness and feeling of the entire group. Hence, when nobody in the groups cares very much about an issue, the leaders probably do not attach much salience. However, if the rank and file become excited about it (or if there is a prospect they will become excited), the issue becomes the most important (salient) thing in the world for the leaders.

Of course, we are not denying the possibility that leaders may have strong opinions about issues even when they have rather low salience because their membership does not care about it very much. Leaders are simply more likely to act on the basis of their opinions when the followers care than when the follow- ers do not care. It also scarcely needs to be mentioned that leaders will have a lot to say about what the rest of the group

ignores or pays attention to. But they will rarely have
monopoly control over salience, which is one of the reasons
group leadership is so wearing -- and politics is so interesting.

For the degree of friendship, neutrality, and hostility
for a particular set of actors you must also frequently rely
on judgment. Look at the tone and style of communications
between any pair of political actors. Are they saying to each
other, "Gee, we get along so well, why don't you do what I
want?" Or are they saying, "If you don't do what I want, I'll
never speak to you again." These two basic styles reflect real
differences in feelings of friendship and hostility between the
actors. When the mother in our Prince family says, "If you
object to my bowling with the girls, I'll go home to mother,"
that's hostility. When the father says, "Sweetheart, because
I bought a new suit, I'll do dishes for a month so you can go
bowling on Thursday nights," that's friendship.

Of course, you cannot always take the friendship-neutrality-
hostility statements at face value. In some cases, friendly
remarks and moderate discussions may cover seething hate. For
that reason, it is necessary for you to examine closely the
factors underlying the relationship between actors. Three
such factors should be looked at in determining whether to
assign a "+," "0," or "-" to the way one actor relates to
another.

One reason for political friendship is that one actor feels
morally or legally responsible to represent the interests and
views of another actor. The most obvious case of this type of
relationship is congressmen and voters in their districts.
Similar cases can be found in the relationship between a supervisor and subordinates and a parent and his or her children.

A second reason for the existence of political friendship,
neutrality, and hostility can be found in the mind set that has
developed the historic patterns of agreement and disagreement
over issues between two actors. Members of a political party
in a legislature often agree with one another on a series of
bills because in the past they have repeatedly found more on
which to agree than to disagree. As a result, they tend to
be political friends. Conversely, members of opposing parties
tend to disagree and tend therefore to be political enemies.
Their hostility is a result of their historic disagreement with
each other. In the family example, the father and grandmother
are unfriendly to one another as a result of a long series of
past disagreements on many issues (such as whether the marriage
between the husband and wife should have taken place).

The final reason that friendship, neutrality, and hostility
patterns develop between two actors is that one actor has something the other one wants. This situation is called "cross-
issue bargaining." A legislature provides a convenient example.
When a bill to support spending in one congressman's district
is being considered, many different legislators will support
it because they know that if they do, the legislator whose
district is being helped is more likely to vote with them when
a bill comes up to help their district. This so-called vote
trading takes place in many different areas besides legislatures.

Providing estimations of political friendship, neutrality,
and hostility between actors is a difficult task. First, you
must ask if the relationship between the two actors is a result
of some moral or legal obligation -- if the relationship is
determined by past agreements or disagreements, or if it is a
result of a cross-issue bargaining relationship. Once this
question is answered, you are prepared to determine whether a
"+," "0," or "-" should go in the appropriate cell. If it is
a moral or legal obligation, it should be a "+." If it is a
result of consistency, the ratio of agreement to disagreement
over the range of past and present issues affecting the two
actors determines whether it is a "+," "0," or "-." If it is
cross-issue bargaining, the relative power and salience of the
respective actors determines whether it is a "+" or a "0."
Precise calculations exist for making these determinations,
but a computer is required to carry them out. For most of your
purposes, you can use the general rules to determine political
friendship, neutrality, or hostility summarized below:

1. If there is a moral or legal obligation, then "+."
2. If past and present issues shape the relationship, then
   a) disagreement more than agreement, "-"
   b) agreement more than disagreement, "+"
   c) relative balance between agreement and disagreement, "0."
3. If there is cross-issue bargaining, then
   a) salience of actor is greater than power of other actor,
      "+"
   b) salience of actor is equal to or less than power of
      other actor, "0."

Although extremely complex to complete, the chart showing
the relationships among political actors is important. By
understanding these relationships in terms of the friendship-
neutrality-hostility concepts we have described above, you can
determine the propensity one actor has to agree with another
regardless of the original actor's predisposition. For example,
we would expect that father could get mother to agree with his
positions on issues more readily than most other family members.
These patterns are relatively stable and therefore can be used
to forecast the degree to which changes in issue position might
occur.

B. <u>Systematic Data Collection from Documentary Sources</u>

So far we have been discussing how to translate your general understanding of a political situation into the numbers, pluses, and minuses of the Prince charts. Many of the situations you will want to study will be situations in which you have a lot of general information, either because of your personal knowledge and involvement or because it is something you have carefully studied by reading books, magazine articles, and newspapers. Therefore, you will often find that you will be able to fill out the charts using the information you have. In analyzing such situations, you might use in an informal way some of the techniques discussed below.

However, you may want to do some new research and information gathering about a situation you don't have a lot of information about and gather the information as systematcially as possible. The rest of this chapter has some pointers for doing this. Keep in mind, however, that even the most precise and systematic research will not help you unless you have a clear idea of what you are gathering the data on. Therefore, keep clearly in mind the first part of this chapter if you try any of the techniques suggested in this section.

<u>Issue position</u>. Public news stories and other accounts of political issues usually have a great deal of information about the IPs (issue positions) of actors. Participants in politics are frequently expressing themselves as being for or against various proposed courses of action. The more consistently an actor states publicly that he or she is for something, the more confidently you can assign a positive IP for that actor. Make sure, however, that the actor states his or her position consistently before many different audiences before you assign an IP. Also look for qualifications in an actor's support or opposition statements. In case no qualifications are ever mentioned, you can assign a +3 or a -3. Depending on how frequently qualifications are mentioned, you should assign a 2 or a 1.

In legislative bodies of various sorts, actors are often called upon to vote and explain their vote on various public issues. These votes can also frequently be used to assign IPs. In still other cases, you can estimate an actor's IP fairly closely simply by knowing the purpose of an intended decision. If its purpose is to make that actor richer, more important, or otherwise help the actor, you don't have to worry too much about assigning a positive IP to the actor on that issue. If, conversely, the decision has a likely result of being harmful to the actor's interests, a negative IP is a good bet.

44

Salience. Salience is a trickier thing to measure. One
thing to look for is how frequently an actor says or does anything about the issue. The more activity, the more salient
the issue probably is to that actor. Somewhat paradoxically,
a lack of activity may sometimes indicate high salience.

The effect on the actor can also be a clue to salience.
The more an actor's interests are affected by a proposed
decision, the more salient it will normally be to him. For
example, a minimum wage law is generally high salience to a
labor union. However, much more salient would be a proposed
law designed to affect the right to strike, which affects the
very raison d'etre of a labor union.

Power. Power is difficult to measure, but it is the most
constant, or slowly changing, component of the Prince System.
Generally speaking, current reports on the dynamics of political situations do not explicitly give information about
power.

In order to estimate power, you will most likely have to
do some background research on the attributes and position of
an actor. Does the actor possess many resources that are
important in determining the way a decision is made? For
example, does he or she control committees, sources of communication, or other important institutions? If the decision has
to do with money, does the actor have a lot of wealth? If the
decision has to do with possible coercion, does the actor
possess a lot of capacity for coercion? Be very careful here
to avoid the "halo effect" which is a weakness in many political analyses. Just because an actor possesses a lot of one
kind of resource doesn't mean that it is powerful on all
issues. The United States, for example, possesses an over-
whelming military power with respect to Canada, but this
hasn't stopped the Canadians from putting severe restrictions
on American investments in their economy.

In trying to measure any of these three variables -- issue
position, salience, and power -- you should develop a list as
you go through your sources. Make a note of each instance of
evidence about one of the three variables. Then put all the
actors in rank order, with the highest on top and the lowest
on the bottom. After doing this, you can usually decide with
a fair degree of confidence which ones to assign a 3, which a
2, which a 1, and which a 0.

Friendship-Neutrality-Hostility. In deciding what scores
to give actors for this chart, history is sometimes a good
source. It may tell you if the two actors usually cooperate
or conflict, and therefore whether to assign a "+" or a "-"
between them. It usually happens that the way the first actor

feels about the second is the way the second will feel about the first. But look out for exceptions to this. Although they are rather infrequent, exceptions can be extremely important as a clue to future issue positions.

The sources you use for the other variables will sometimes also contain information about friendly relations between two actors, or even formal pacts and alliances. This can be very useful in filling out the Friendship-Neutrality-Hostility chart.

In case you have some other applications, particularly after reading through the case studies in the Appendix, some blank charts and a political map are included at the end of this chapter.

PRINCE CHART

ISSUE: _____

(State in terms of a desired political outcome, using a phrase beginning with a verb.)

ACTORS	ISSUE POSITION	X	POWER	X	SALIENCE	=	TOTAL SUPPORT BY ACTOR
	-3-0-+3		1-3		1-3		
		X		X		=	
		X		X		=	
		X		X		=	
		X		X		=	
		X		X		=	
		X		X		=	
		X		X		=	
		X		X		=	

Totals:
A - Scores of all actors supporting the issue: ___
B - Absolute value of actors opposing the issue: ___
C - Scores of actors with zero issue positions: ___
D - Totals A, B, C: ___
E - Total A + 1/2 of Total C: ___

Probability of Support = $\frac{E}{D}$ = _____

FRIENDSHIP-NEUTRALITY-HOSTILITY CHART

This Actor feels about this Actor:

_____ _____ _____ _____ _____ _____

_____

_____

_____

_____

_____

_____

Key: + Actor is friendly

      - Actor is enemy

      0 Actor is neutral

48

PRINCE POLITICAL MAP

ISSUE: _____

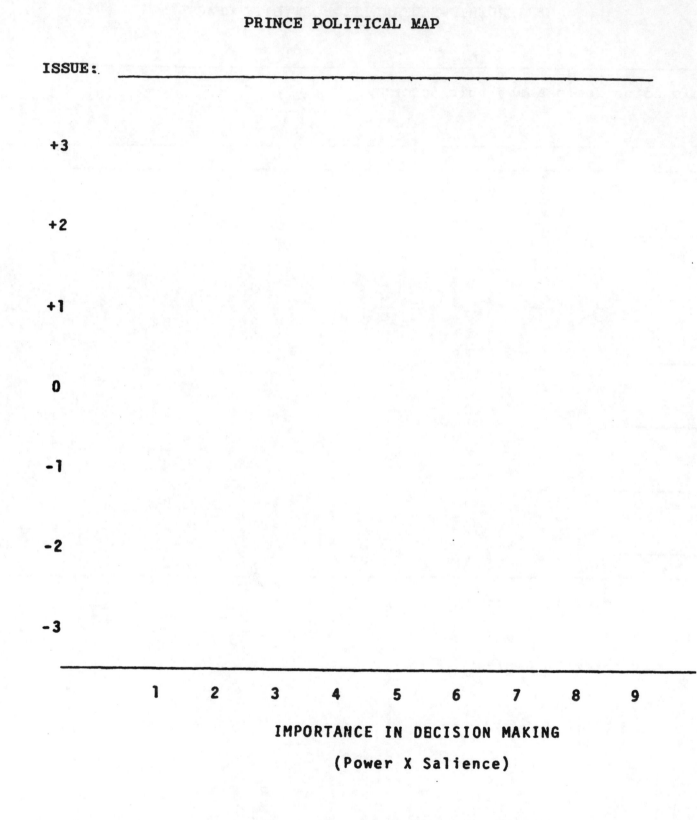

ISSUE POSITION

+3

+2

+1

0

-1

-2

-3

1   2   3   4   5   6   7   8   9

IMPORTANCE IN DECISION MAKING

(Power X Salience)

APPENDIX: THREE CASE STUDIES

STUDY 1: HOW THE PRINCE SYSTEM PRODUCED THE AMERICAN CONSTITUTION

One of the mysteries of the American Constitutional Convention is why George Washington remained so passive during its sessions yet emerged from the convention as the first American political superstar. It can now be revealed that Washington was not passive at all, but was very actively, if quietly, applying a PRINCE analysis to what was happening. Many people then—and now—have thought that Washington was just another pretty face without any political skills to match his military successes. It has been argued that in politics he was just a front man for clever Machiavellian politicians. The truth of the matter is that he was himself a skillful politician employing the appropriate PRINCE charts at every occasion. Washington earned the title "father of his country," by first becoming every American's Prince.

In fewer than four months about forty men wrote a document that was a masterpiece and resolved the differences of a diverse collection of anti-British rebels who had only just begun to develop a conception of an American nation. Such a document was not produced before 1787, nor has one been produced since. At least one good explanation for what is universally ranked as one of the wonders of the political world is that someone was working the PRINCE accounting system. It seems clear to us that it had to be Washington, with his experience as a surveyor and his familiarity with using charts to get the lay of the land. While the rest of the guys were boozing it up in the Indian Queen, a local pub, on the evening of May 27, 1787, Washington was busy in his room with four empty PRINCE accounting system charts.

His first job was to reduce the forty-odd delegates to a manageable number of political actors. His limit, as we indicated in the first chapter, was ten political actors.

He was helped in this task first by the rules of the convention that provided for voting by state delegations rather than individuals. He had to deal with only twelve actors—the thirteen former colonies minus Rhode Island, whose delegates boycotted the meeting. This was probably close enough to the ideal upper limit of ten, but because it was summer Washington looked for other ways to make his job easier by reducing the number of actors.

> **PRINCiple 3.1:** *   To simplify the PRINCE charts, lump together actors who have strong common interests.

For the sake of simplicity, George Washington lumped the actors together. Washington called South Carolina, North Carolina, and Georgia the *Deep South*. The Deep South states had similar economic interests that were different from those of the North, including most significantly a reliance upon slave labor. Therefore Washington expected, quite rightly, that they would act together on a wide range of issues. George called New Jersey, Delaware, Connecticut, New York, and Maryland the *States' Righters*. The States' Righters were small states worried about their continued influence in any new arrangements, plus New York, a majority of whose delegates also worried about states' rights because they wanted a weak central government. George treated Massachusetts and New Hampshire as one. These two states also had similar economic interests, plus a long background of cultural affinity and close cooperation between their citizens. There were only two states treated separately—Pennsylvania, the state of Ben Franklin, and George's own state, Virginia. Washington thus ended up with five actors: (1) the Deep South, (2) the States' Righters, (3) Massachusetts-New Hampshire, (4) Pennsylvania, and (5) Virginia.

After defining the actors, George got out his PRINCE charts and went to the next problem—identifying issues. The first issue was whether the convention would try to make the thirteen states into one nation or just strengthen their existing alliance against England. The convention had been organized for the official purpose of amending the old constitution, the Articles of Confederation. But Washington and some of the other leaders, like Benjamin Franklin, thought that the old constitution was such a mess that an entirely new one should be written.

*Look for these inserts throughout the case studies in each section. They summarize important points made by the case.

They also wanted a new constitution so that the thirteen states could be bound into one nation. Thus Issue 1 was whether the convention should write an entirely new constitution that would create a nation or amend the old constitution that would simply make the existing confederation stronger.

PRINCiple 3.2:   Identify issues in terms of relatively specific outcomes.

The second major issue was how strong the federal executive should be. A few delegates like Alexander Hamilton wanted a king, but most of the delegates had had their stomachs full of kings. So Issue 2 was whether they would have a strong executive by electing one person for a reasonable period of time (at least four years or more) or a weak executive by electing more than one person for a short period of time.

Related to this question was a third issue—how the executive (the president) was to be elected. Those who favored a strong executive wanted election by the people. Others, however, opposed this procedure and wanted the president elected by the states or, in a few cases, by the Congress. So Issue 3 was whether the president would be elected by the people.

Another set of issues had to do with the legislature. First was the question of *how* the states should be represented in Congress. The delegates from the larger states wanted congressional seats distributed according to the proportion of the population in each state. Of course the delegates from the small states weren't stupid; they knew that if representation was based on population they would always be outvoted. Therefore they opposed proportional representation and wanted each state to have the same number of seats. Washington saw that the question of proportional representation in the legislature would be Issue 4.

If the states were going to be represented by population, however, a question would arise whether slaves would be counted as people and thereby increase the population of the slave states. The question of counting slaves became Washington's Issue 5.

Two issues had to do with the powers of Congress, in particular whether Congress would have the power to (1) tax exports and (2) regulate the slave trade. The latter boiled down to whether Congress would abolish the slave trade. These two issues were 6 and 7 respectively.

Because many of the delegates had been forced to read Montesquieu when they were students, they became obsessed with the idea that a good government needed an executive, a legislature, and a judiciary.

Although there was a consensus that there should be a supreme court in the capital, not all agreed that there should be federal courts in the states. Hence, Issue 8 was whether the federal courts should operate within states.

Realizing that the delegates would probably spend most of the beautiful summer of 1787 cooped up indoors debating these eight substantive issues, George knew that they would still have two very important procedural issues left: (1) how the Constitution was to be amended and (2) how the Constitution was to be ratified. Having gotten wind of the scuttlebut from the delegates, Washington knew that amending the Constitution would be Issue 9—whether the delegates would accept a proposed amendment procedure that allowed the Constitution to be amended by three-fourths of the states or would favor some other plan such as unanimous consent by all the states, which would in effect give each state a veto.

Washington's final issue dealt with the ratification process. He defined Issue 10 as the ratification of the Constitution by the people rather than by the states through their legislatures.

Washington could have defined a number of other issues, but he felt that these gave him enough of an idea of the major disputes and results of the convention. He then made a list of the ten issues and a label for each issue that he would use on his PRINCE charts. The list was:

1. The purpose of the convention is to write a new constitution and thereby create a nation. Label: *Nation.*
2. A strong executive will be created. Label: *Exec.*
3. People shall elect the president. Label: *Presid.*
4. Representation in the legislature will be according to population. Label: *Legis.*
5. Slaves will be counted as part of a state's population. Label: *Slaves.*
6. Congress will have the power to tax exports. Label: *Exports.*
7. Congress will have the power to regulate, and hence to abolish, the slave trade. Label: *Slave Trade.*
8. Federal courts shall be established in the states. Label: *Courts.*
9. Only three-fourths of the states are needed to amend the Constitution. Label: *Amend.*
10. Ratification of the Constitution by the people. Label: *Ratif.*

Having identified the basic issues as well as the primary political actors, Washington now had the columns and rows of the four PRINCE

CHART 3–1. Political actors' issue positions.

Actors	Issues				
	Nation	*Exec.*	*Presid.*	*Legis.*	*Slaves*
Deep South (Ga., S.C., N.C.)	+3	+3	+2	+3	+3
States' Righters (N.Y., N.J., Del., Conn., Md.)	–3	–1	–3	–3	–2
Massachusetts-New Hampshire	+3	+3	+3	0	–3
Pennsylvania	+3	+3	+3	–3	–3
Virginia	+3	0	+3	+3	+3
	Exports	*Slave trade*	*Courts*	*Amend.*	*Ratif.*
Deep South (Ga., S.C., N.C.)	–3	–3	–3	–3	+3
States' Righters (N.Y., N.J., Del., Conn., Md.)	+2	+2	–2	–2	+1
Massachusetts-New Hampshire	0	+2	+3	+3	+3
Pennsylvania	+2	+2	+3	+2	+3
Virginia	–3	+2	+3	+2	+2

charts labeled. He then proceeded to estimate the numbers necessary to fill up the cells of the charts.

> **PRINCiple 3.3:** Use the PRINCE system to project the voting decisions of legislative bodies.

He started with the issue position—Chart 3–1. He scored a +3 when there was agreement among the members of the coalitions for a particular formulation and –3 when there was agreement against it. When there was not full agreement, he scored somewhere between 1 and 3, depending upon how strong a consensus was for or against the proposal among each coalition-actor.

Washington then moved on to Chart 3–2—the power of each actor for each issue. He gave each group a power of 1, except the States' Righters, whom he gave a power of 2. He thus employed an abbreviated form of Chart 3–2.

The information in Chart 3–3 proved critical for Washington and the American Constitutional Convention because it registered the salience of the issues for each of the actors. Chart 3–3 indicates the importance Washington thought each of the actors had for each of the issues. One can see how critical salience is by first multiplying Charts 3–1 and

CHART 3-2. Power of the actors on issues.

Actors	Power for all issues
Deep South (Ga., S.C., N.C.)	1
States' Righters (N.Y., N.J., Del., Conn., Md.)	2
Massachusetts-New Hampshire	1
Pennsylvania	1
Virginia	1

3-2 and comparing the product to Charts 3-1, 3-2, and 3-3 multiplied together. Chart 3-4 presents the sums of the columns, which is an indicator of what is likely to happen.

If salience were not figured into the PRINCE system, Washington would have been particularly despondent. Without salience, there seems to be only clearcut support for the ratification procedure and a strong executive. All the rest of the figures are borderline. However, the addition of salience indicates a strong commitment for creating a union, a strong executive, counting slaves as population, and the amendment and ratification procedures. There also appears to be a strong commitment against a legislature based on a proportion of the population and the power of Congress to tax exports.

PRINCiple 3.4: Always remember to consider salience when making a compromise. It's frequently prudent to offer a little extra to the side with the higher salience.

Washington assumed that 20 points was a cutoff for consensus on an issue (+ for and - against) and concluded that a large number of compromises would be necessary to produce a strong constitution. Realizing the need for compromise, he formulated a strategy on his part that would keep any single political actor from pulling out of the convention. To help him do this, he completed Chart 3-5 of the PRINCE system.

Washington was particularly wary of *polarization*, a phenomenon that has rendered many meetings and some political systems hopelessly confused. Polarization is the degree to which the political actors are split into two opposing camps. The degree to which there are no actors in the system who are friendly with the enemies of other actors is an

CHART 3-3. Salience of actors on issues.

Actors	Issues				
	Nation	*Exec.*	*Presid.*	*Legis.*	*Slaves*
Deep South					
(Ga., S.C., N.C.)	3	2	1	2	3
States' Righters					
(N.Y., N.J., Del., Conn., Md.)	2	3	2	3	1
Massachusetts-New Hampshire	3	2	1	3	1
Pennsylvania	3	2	1	3	1
Virginia	3	3	1	3	3
	Exports	*Slave trade*	*Courts*	*Amend.*	*Ratif.*
Deep South					
(Ga., S.C., N.C.)	3	3	3	1	1
States' Righters					
(N.Y., N.J., Del., Conn., Md.)	3	1	2	1	1
Massachusetts-New Hampshire	3	1	2	3	1
Pennsylvania	2	1	3	3	1
Virginia	3	0	3	3	2

indication of polarization. In contrast, the degree to which friends and enemies are thoroughly mixed indicates a basically depolarized system.

> PRINCiple 3.5: Polarization is destructive and consensus is constructive if you are on the side of the consensus. If you are not, the converse is true.

Washington employed a simple procedure for calculating the polarization level of the convention. He ranked all pairs of actors at the convention as friendly, neutral, or hostile. Chart 3-6 indicates how the political actors were ordered.

Washington breathed a sigh of relief when he examined the list. He discovered that the actors were relatively depolarized, because Virginia as well as Massachusetts-New Hampshire provided friendly links between most of the hostile pairs. The major threat of polarization came from the fact that the States' Righters group was hostile toward both Pennsylvania and Virginia and the Deep South was also hostile towards Pennsylvania. This situation created the possibility of two camps forming—one around Pennsylvania and Virginia and the other around the Deep South and States' Righters. Although the situation was relatively depolarized at the outset, conditions existed for hostility be-

CHART 3–4. Predicted issue outcomes with and without salience.

	Issues				
	Nation	Exec.	Presid.	Legis.	Slaves
Charts 3-1 X 3-2 (Without Salience)	+6	+7	+5	-3	-4
Charts 3-1 X 3-2 X 3-3 (With Salience)	+24	+12	+5	-12	+8
	Exports	Slave trade	Courts	Amend.	Ratif.
Charts 3-1 X 3-2 (Without Salience)	0	+7	+2	0	+13
Charts 3-1 X 3-2 X 3-3 (With Salience)	-2	-1	+7	+14	+15

CHART 3–5. Friendship-neutrality-hostility chart.

This actor	Feels about this actor:				
	Deep South	States' Righters	Massachusetts-New Hampshire	Pennsylvania	Virginia
Deep South		-	-	-	+
States' Righters	-		+	-	-
Massachusetts-New Hampshire	-	+	·	+	-
Pennsylvania	-	-	+		+
Virginia	+	-	-	+	

tween the two potential camps to grow and for the convention to fail as a result of that growth.

Fortunately, Washington had a couple of things going for him. One of the most important was that he was a member of the prestigious Virginia delegation. Realizing that he was something of a national hero, he concluded that if he took public positions and got involved directly in the issues, he would generate a break between the camps. He concluded that his role was to be passive in public and at formal meetings but to work actively for compromise behind the scenes. He could also keep Virginia from antagonizing the States' Righters if he played a consensus-building role.

Washington also was fortunate to have Benjamin Franklin in the Pennsylvania delegation. By far, Benjamin was *the* star of the con-

58

CHART 3–6. Pairs of actors ordered from friendly to neutral to hostile.

Pair of actors	Friendship-neutrality-hostility score
Pennsylvania-Virginia	+
Pennsylvania-Massachusetts/New Hampshire	+
Deep South-Virginia	+
States' Righters-Massachusetts/New Hampshire	+
Deep South-Massachusetts/New Hampshire	–
Virginia-Massachusetts/New Hampshire	–
Deep South-States' Righters	–
Deep South-Pennsylvania	–
Pennsylvania-States' Righters	–
Virginia-States' Righters	–

vention which meant that Pennsylvania delegates would follow his lead and that delegations from other states would be open to his views. Washington got to him before the convention and convinced him (we are not sure whether he used the PRINCE system or just appealed to Franklin's enormous ego) to modify Pennsylvania's view and to seek compromise with the other states.

Another fortunate factor that operated to the advantage of those who wanted a successful convention was that the States' Righters and the Deep South had a moderate degree of antagonism toward each other. Washington's plan—to make sure that the two groups did not form a coalition against the rest of the actors—was greatly aided by the basic antagonism the two groups had for each other. It was not a sufficiently strong antagonism to prevent them from cooperating (as was, for example, the antagonism between Virginia and the States' Righters) but it was sufficient to prevent the two groups from joining together and wrecking the convention.

> PRINCiple 3.6: Compromise occurs on issues about which there is no consensus if actors have a consensus on other issues.

The charts helped Washington in many ways. For example, he could see that the strong executive (Issue 2) was uncertain of victory. The favorable actors—Deep South, Massachusetts-New Hampshire, and Pennsylvania—had only six votes (out of twelve). Washington's own state,

CHART 3–7. Score sheet comparing the PRINCE system to actual results.

	PRINCE analysis of events most likely to occur	
Issue	*PRINCE total score*	*Actual results*
1 *(Nation)*	+24	Occurred as stated
10 *(Ratif.)*	+15	Occurred as stated
9 *(Amend.)*	+14	Occurred as stated
2 *(Exec.)*	+12	Occurred as stated
5 *(Slaves)*	+8	Occurred but with slaves counting as three-fifths
8 *(Courts)*	+7	Compromise by leaving to Congress to decide
3 *(Presid.)*	+5	Compromise using electoral college instead of people
7 *(Slave Trade)*	–1	No regulating until 1808
6 *(Exports)*	–2	Rejected as stated
4 *(Legis.)*	–12	Most highly debated issue with a 50-50 compromise effected

Virginia, was so evenly divided that the delegation frequently was dead-locked and was unable to vote. (Note that Virginia has a zero issue position, but a saliency of 3 on this issue.) The idea was to get some of the States' Righters, who were only moderately opposed, to support a strong executive. As he looked at his friendship-neutrality-hostility chart he could see that it would be very unwise for anyone from Pennsylvania or the Deep South to lobby for a strong executive. The States' Righters had hostility toward both Pennsylvania and the Deep South. However, the Massachusetts-New Hampshire group was viewed more positively by the States' Righters, so Washington knew that they would be more likely to listen favorably to appeals from one of the New England delegation.

Washington also used his PRINCE calculations to plan where and how to make compromises that led to a successful consensus. On the question whether to count slaves as part of the population, it was clear that some compromise would have to be made. At first Washington thought of proposing to split the difference and count slaves as one-half, which is a common bargaining strategy. But he looked at the salience figures and saw that the proponents of counting slaves, the Deep South and Virginia, held their view with higher salience than the opponents who did not want to count slaves at all. So he suggested giving the South and Virginia slightly more than half and counting slaves as three-fifths of the population—bizarre from a humanistic viewpoint, but quite sound politically. On the other hand, when Washington looked at the salience for how legislative representation should be based (Issue 4) he saw that both sides held their views with equally high salience. Therefore he was attracted to the notion—which was finally accepted—of having two houses of the legislature, one to satisfy the views of each side.

It should also be clear that the decisions made by the convention rarely placed the States' Righters and the Deep South on the same side. A decision not to count slaves but to use proportional representation for determining representatives to the legislature would have done this. Instead, there was a compromise on both issues so that neither side would be alienated.

Another strategy followed by the convention was to avoid certain critical issues. Hence, the decision to end the importation of slaves was not to take effect until 1808—twenty-one years after the convention—and the question of the role of the federal courts was to be dealt with in the Congress itself.

Two of the time-worn patterns of compromise appeared to be most important here: One is to give each party half of the pie, which was implemented in the decisions on proportional representation and counting slaves, and the other is to postpone the consequence of the decision, if not the decision itself.

The PRINCE system gave Washington a picture of the areas of conflict and the actors most likely to disagree. As Table 3-7 shows, it forecast the convention results with notable accuracy. From this picture he was able to create an atmosphere of compromise by playing a quiet and unifying public role and a private role that worked for compromise. Fortunately for him and the new union, the predispositions of the actors were basically in the direction with which Washington agreed, which allowed him to play a consensus role in dealing with the convention. As we will see in the next chapter, it is sometimes necessary for those using the PRINCE system to play the role of breaking up existing agreements to get basic change. During the Constitutional Convention, Washington had only to insure an atmosphere of trust and compromise to achieve his purposes.

STUDY 2: BOBBY PLANTER VS. THE BUREAUCRAT
-- A PRINCE ANALYSIS

There once was a very bright young Ph.D. named Bobby Planter who went to work for the Department of Housing of the State of California. Dr. Planter began his job one Monday morning in August of 1969. He had just received his Ph.D. in modern housing, an exciting and innovative interdisciplinary program offered by Southern State Normal University. Planter had graduated *cum laude* from Harvard with a B.A. in economics in 1966 and had chosen SSNU because it had the best (not to mention the only) Ph.D. program in modern housing. His curriculum had drawn upon the departments of economics, geography, bricklaying, public administration, and law. All his coursework and research (including a dissertation) were focused on one concern—delivering better housing for less money to Americans, especially poor Americans.

The night before Planter was to start working he was paid a visit by Dr. Lyle Stuart, also a young Ph.D., who was leaving the Department of Housing. Dr. Stuart was moving to greener pastures by taking a job with the Department of Urban Planning in Little Rock, Arkansas. After a few drinks, Stuart told Planter that the California Department of Housing was filled with typical bureaucrats who, as anyone knows, are afraid of their own shadows and who talk in incomprehensible riddles filled with uninterpretable jargon. Stuart recounted at least a dozen instances when he had identified the proper strategy to solve a particular problem but was thwarted by the bureaucrats' overconcern with the politicians, the public, the budget, and their superiors. He illustrated in graphic terms how every suggestion he made was ignored, treated as an "interesting recommendation," or viewed as an occasion for a study committee.

PRINCiple 7.1: Bureaucrats have to operate in a situation in which their power is low.

Of course, Planter had already expected this. His public administration professor at SSNU was a brilliant thirty-year-old full professor who had attained wisdom during a six-month career in government. He taught his students the latest in administrative techniques, including cost-benefit analysis and permanent sensitivity training. This professor had unsuccessfully tried to organize a graduate public administration program at SSNU, had failed to implement his administrative training practices in several state governments, and had been frustrated in an attempt to reorganize the curriculum of public administration at SSNU. In fact, there was probably no one within a thousand miles whose failures in dealing with bureaucracies made him so well qualified to teach public administration.

This expert professor could describe in great detail the conservatism and imbecility of bureaucrats, and he thoroughly tested his students, including Planter, on their ability to understand the "bureaucratic condition." Hence, Planter was well prepared for his job—which is to say that he expected the worst. Stuart's visit only served to reinforce Planter's expertise on the nature of modern bureaucracy.

During the first week of his job, Planter discovered (with some unhappiness—and a great deal of relief) that the interpretation supplied by his public administration professor and confirmed by Stuart was absolutely correct. He confirmed his notions by using the world-famous participant-observation techniques developed at SSNU ("snooping with a moral purpose," as his public administration professor had called it). For example, Planter witnessed an assistant to Harvey Lowe, the head of the Department of Housing, refuse to approve a trip by a departmental employee to Los Angeles to investigate housing problems on the grounds that the mayor of Los Angeles would consider it meddling. "Better people should live in rat-infested housing than the mayor should be a little ruffled," thought Planter.

From that time on, Planter resolved to do his share to rectify at least one obvious cause of malaise in the United States: incompetent public administration. The opportunity to carry out his pledge was not long in coming. In the second week of September, Harvey Lowe announced that the very next week there would be a high-level departmental meeting to discuss how to encourage the use of more efficient home-building methods and materials in the Los Angeles area. Planter was especially eager for this meeting. He had written his Ph.D. dissertation on the use of new building methods and materials in Plattsburg, New York. So he was sure he could use his expertise effectively to intervene at the meeting and begin to change the archaic bureaucratic processes that dominated the Department of Housing.

He labored all weekend to develop a comprehensive plan to promote the use of new building techniques and materials in Los Angeles. He studied the building codes, the local and state laws, the existing practices, and the nature of businesses and unions in the local construction industry. He relied upon all the interdisciplinary skills he had developed at SSNU. He certainly would have received at least an A- from the director of the Ph.D. program in modern housing.

The meeting started fifteen minutes late because the deputy chief of the department was slow in brewing the coffee. The delay only served to strengthen Planter's resolve. Finally, Lowe opened the discussion by identifying the problem. He said there was some evidence that a three-bedroom house could be built and sold at a reasonable profit for about $22,000 if all of the newest techniques and materials were used. He continued by estimating that given the kinds of materials and techniques presently in use, the best price for a comparable house in the Los Angeles area was $29,000. The primary reason for the meeting was to develop a strategy to bring the prices of houses closer to the lower figure.

Planter took the floor as soon as Lowe finished speaking. First, he pointed out that his calculations led him to believe the gap was wider— $21,000 using the new techniques versus $32,000 using existing methods. Nevertheless, even if Lowe were correct (which in Planter's mind was highly doubtful because Lowe had majored in English literature rather than in modern housing), something had to be done. Planter continued by saying that the situation was deplorable given the available technologies. He advocated a concerted attack on the problem through the following actions:

1. A public statement by the governor calling for more efficient methods and materials in the housing industry
2. The establishment of a uniform state-wide set of building codes based upon the guidelines set by the federal government's Department of Housing and Urban Development
3. A $300,000,000 program to train contractors and skilled laborers in the use of the new techniques and materials
4. The creation of a watchdog committee to monitor building in the Los Angeles area. This committee would be staffed

by local citizens—consumers—and members of the State Housing Department. Its job would be to identify publicly those builders who refused to adopt the new methods and procedures.

Planter presented his arguments with perfectly constructed charts and graphs. He projected that by following his plan it would be reasonable to expect that within two years the average cost of a three-bedroom house would be down approximately to $24,000 (this sum represents adjustment for the inflationary dollar).

Planter looked around him as he finished his talk and saw that the group was visibly stunned. The other six members, including Lowe (who had by now consumed four cups of coffee), sat nervously listening. It seemed to Planter several minutes before anyone spoke. The first person to break the silence was the same assistant who had refused to sign the travel authorization the first week Planter was there. He was a fifty-year-old man who giggled nervously and was extremely polite— the kind of guy you would never want to borrow money from. His name was Mortimer LaStrange, and he had been born a bureaucrat.

PRINCiple 7.2: Technical knowledge must be used skillfully before it can give power to political actors.

LaStrange started out by congratulating Planter for prividing such a stimulating program of ideas. He was so impressed with the ideas that he proposed the immediate establishment of an interdepartmental committee from the half-dozen or so agencies that LaStrange identified as being concerned with Planter's proposed course of action. This committee could thoroughly explore the merits of Planter's ideas, said LaStrange, and, in his giggling words, "do some fine tuning on our young friend's already fine thoughts."

At first, Planter was pleased and more than a little surprised. However, the impact of the flattery soon wore off, and he remembered what his public administration professor and Lyle Stuart had told him. "My God!" he said to himself. "Here we go again, using committees to kill innovative ideas." LaStrange continued even while Planter was trying to recover. He argued in his beautiful bureaucratic style that the problem was "multifaceted" and that a large number of private and public interests were involved. He suggested that an advisory commission be set up with members drawn from various groups including the Los Angeles mayor's office, local union and construction industry groups, companies producing the new techniques and methods, and members of the Housing Department. This committee would make recommendations to Lowe relating to the issues raised by Planter after a thorough study. He proposed that the committee be called "The Southern California Ad Hoc Advisory Commission on Building Methods in Housing and Other Construction."

By now Planter was horrified. He had witnessed first-hand the incredible stupidity of bureaucrats; worse yet, he had seen the perversion of his own carefully framed ideas. Planter was even more crushed when, before he could reply, Lowe excused himself from the room, saying either that he had to talk with the governor or had to play golf (Planter wasn't sure which) and placing LaStrange in charge of the meeting. His final words were that "Mortimer seems to have everything under control." Although Planter had not been in the bureaucracy long enough to be infected with the common disease of paranoia, he did start to wonder whether LaStrange and Lowe had previously discussed the matter and if they were secretly conniving with the building industry and the unions.

Bobby Planter and Mortimer LaStrange have presented two sharply contrasting styles for lowering the cost of housing. Bobby's method is to launch a frontal attack on the vested interests that profit from the high cost of construction, including the men in power, frequently in local communities, who tacitly accept industry practices that are costly to the consumer. LaStrange's plan, from Planter's point of view, reeked of compromise from the very start. LaStrange first proposed the establishment of a study committee, which is a time-honored device to slow down action (while people have to wait for the study committee to do its studying) and also greatly increases the chances of watering down the proposed action by compromise (because the delay and the forum of the study committee will increase the chances of conflicting points of view being effectively put forward). The advisory commission will tend toward the same outcomes, plus some additional ones equally distasteful from Planter's viewpoint. The advisory commission was to be composed of labor and business groups that would undoubtedly be hostile to the proposed policy. This device, bringing in opponents of a policy to help plan it, is as old as bureaucracies. It has a name: cooptation. It is based on the principle, which usually holds true, that people who are associated with the early stages of policy making—especially on an "insider" basis—are very likely to be in favor of the policy, or at least moderate in their opposition. Once again, of course, the price paid for such a strategy is dealing, compromise, and the inevitable tailoring of policy, to some degree at least, in the direction of the groups engaged as advisors.

> **PRINCiple 7.3:** Cooptation is a strategy required when
> one is dealing with more powerful actors.

Which strategy is better, the head-on confrontation of the radical innovator or the slow and easy probings of the old-time bureaucrat? A simple and reasonable question, but one that is never answered in the actual world of daily politics. The reason it is never answered is that human beings can't experiment by trying competing solutions to the same political problems: Trying one solution always changes the situation and the problem. The psychologists can put rats through different mazes under different conditions of reward and punishment to see what happens, but human situations cannot be treated this way. (If for no other reason than no one has yet put up the money to build mazes big enough to fit humans.)

However, this is no longer a problem. PRINCE, if not quite the better mousetrap, does in fact serve as a simulated maze through which we can symbolically make the actors in our story run. The first time through we will set up our simulated maze in the way that LaStrange preferred it; after that we will run the players through according to Bobby Planter's wishes. And finally, we will dredge up our old friends, the PRINCE charts, to show why the people involved scurry through their little paths as they do.

LaStrange's Maze*

LaStrange was appointed chairman of The Southern California Ad Hoc Advisory Commission on Building Methods in Housing and Other Construction. This commission was organized after several meetings of the interdepartmental committee where the time was taken up almost exclusively by exchanges of ever-decreasing cordiality between Planter and LaStrange. Despite their differences, LaStrange invited Planter to be on the commission, along with an old bureaucratic hack who had once been an elected official of a labor union; these three represented the Department of Housing. LaStrange also appointed the legislative assistant of a Los Angeles area state senator who was suspected of re-

*As you might suppose, the authors, being academics, did not write most of this book. Wherever possible, we assigned term papers that could be turned into appropriate chapters. However, the following sections were drafted while graduate students were on their annual spring Beer Bust and Rally Against Inequality and thus were unavailable. Consequently, we fed the numbers from the PRINCE charts into a computer, which produced the following two scenarios.

ceiving large donations from construction companies. In addition, he appointed a member of the Los Angeles mayor's staff, a local building trade union leader, and the owner of the biggest construction company in the area. Finally, LaStrange recruited the vice-president of Kwiki Homes, Inc., a leading supply company in developing more efficient building materials and techniques.

The first meeting took place in February of 1970. In a series of successive monologues each individual said his piece about the housing industry in the Los Angeles area. The union official and the owner of the construction company complained about governmental interference in private enterprise. The mayor's assistant said that the building codes and practices were really a matter that the local building inspectors could handle. Planter chastised the construction industry and the building unions for their reactionary attitudes and their disregard of the consumer. The legislative assistant said that the state should do more for the building industry and promised his senator's support of building subsidies and more liberal home loans. Finally, the vice-president from Kwiki Homes, Inc. talked about exciting new techniques and materials that could revolutionize home building, increase both productivity and profits, and provide a demand for more skilled labor.

By the time the speeches were complete, there was little time left for a discussion of what the committee should do. The muted threats of the local businessman, labor, and the mayor's assistant that the committee should be eliminated were covered up by a coughing spell LaStrange developed right after the speech of the mayor's assistant. LaStrange simply assumed that there was going to be a second meeting and suggested a date. After an hour's hassling over the time and place of the next meeting, there was agreement and the first meeting ended.

The second meeting was different from the first. Most of the members of the committee began calling each other by their first names, and except for Planter were quite friendly. As they entered the room, a janitor was placing a 16-mm projector on a table in front of a screen. LaStrange started the meeting by explaining that the vice-president from Kwiki Homes, Inc. had brought a film explaining the new techniques and materials. Although it was not on the agenda, LaStrange inquired whether or not it would be appropriate to start the meeting by watching the film. Planter objected on the grounds that it was an attempt to slow down the work of the committee. But LaStrange ignored him and went right on talking. The vice-president—whom Planter considered an ally—gave him such a stare that he stopped protesting. Also, the projector and screen were placed so that one person had no seat. This meant that if the film were not shown right away, the projector and screen would have to be completely put away.

PRINCiple 7.4:   Discuss procedure when there are strong differences among participants on a committee.

Everyone was impressed by the content of the film, particularly the owner of the construction firm. There was a spirited discussion of how these techniques and approaches could be more fully exploited in the Los Angeles area. A proposal was developed to establish a set of objectives that local and state government, business, and labor could simultaneously pursue. However, time ran short before there was any definition of specific objectives.

The third meeting was never held. Everyone but LaStrange and the other bureaucratic hack said he could not make it. Planter boycotted the meeting to show his displeasure at its slow pace, and the other people said they had more pressing business. In spite of what Planter perceived to be the failure of LaStrange in strategy, the following events took place:

1. By the end of 1971, minor revisions in local housing codes were implemented to allow the use of some of the newer materials and techniques.
2. For the first time in history the price of a three-bedroom house in the Los Angeles area did not rise during a twelve-month period (June 1970–July 1971).
3. A modest increase in the production of low-cost housing had occurred in the Los Angeles area during 1971.

PRINCiple 7.5:   If the purpose of a committee is to educate its members so they will change their issue position, the death of the committee might represent success.

In addition, LaStrange had submitted a report of the commission (produced totally by his staff) calling for small grants to help retrain workers in the use of the new materials and techniques. This report became the basis for legislation submitted by the senator whose legislative assistant had been on the commission. Although there was still a great gap between the real and the ideal in the price of building a three-bedroom house, LaStrange had helped to create some conditions for ultimate improvement.

Planter's Maze

Bobby Planter began by drafting a public statement to be issued by the governor's office. The statement called for improvement in the productivity of the housing industry. The speech was to be made at a special news conference and publicized as widely as possible. When the governor's staff assistant—who was an undergraduate intern—was approached with the proposal, he told Planter that he ought to take some more political science courses—or maybe take his first one. Why, he said, should the governor spotlight the ills of that particular industry? It was not his role to increase the productivity of industries. The intern said that he wouldn't even send the request to the governor. Planter tried, with no success, to talk to someone else in the governor's office. (When Planter complained to Lowe about the incident, Lowe fumed about the incompetence of the governor's staff and promised to look into the matter. Needless to say, Planter never heard anything of it again.)

PRINCiple 7.6: Access to actual actors is often difficult.

Undaunted, Planter developed a uniform state-wide building code and showed it to the legislative assistant of California's most liberal state senator. The assistant told Planter that although his boss thoroughly approved of the idea, it would never get through the legislature because the power of the building industry and labor unions was so great. Moreover, the local municipalities would fight the move. As a result, there was no cooperation in the legislative branch.

The proposal for a large program to educate contractors and retrain laborers was rejected as premature at every point in the government. Such a program without federal subsidy had no chance of success during the period of tight state budgets that characterized the early 1970s. Moreover, many people questioned the idea of a program that would subsidize those building industries that were producing newer products and techniques. The fact that the questioning emanated from those lobbies that were supported by older building firms and by labor made little difference. There was, consequently, no attempt at legislation of this type.

Finally, the proposal for a watchdog committee to enlist consumer pressure on the building industry was rejected by Harvey Lowe. Lowe's compulsive desire to avoid confrontations of any sort led him to tell Planter that although the idea was sound, there were "constraints operating to limit its feasibility" (a bureaucratic phrase meaning "I'm scared to do it"). There was no development of any type of committee that would generate communication among the interested parties.

By this time, Planter was convinced that it was impossible to get the needed action by the California bureaucracy. His plans were obviously rejected because the bureaucrats were too insecure and too jaded to try anything new, he thought. For that reason, when the University of Southeastern Alaska's Department of Urban Housing offered him a professorship (at a salary 50 percent higher than what he was getting from California) he resigned his post in the Housing Department. Sitting in the airport waiting for his flight to Ketchikan, Planter read the newspaper. One story that caught his eye was headlined:

HOME PRICES UP 10% OVER LAST YEAR

The Two Styles Compared

The skilled student of PRINCE should already have begun to understand the reasons for Planter's failure and LaStrange's ability to produce, if not spectacular success, at least something more than failure. Planter ignored every implication of the PRINCE system; LaStrange followed those implications as if by instinct.* To check on how accurate your guesses are (which is to say how close your guesses are to the authors'), let's briefly look at the strategies of the two men in PRINCE terms.

We will examine the issue position, power, and salience of the actors for the issue of improving cost-efficiency in the building industry of Los Angeles. Chart 7-1 indicates that the overall net opposition to the issue comes primarily from the labor unions. The second most powerful group, the building industry, is not totally convinced that it would be in its interest to push for low-cost methods. It is also apparent that the lack of power and salience among the governor, the mayor, and the consumer makes their positions rather peripheral.

The friendship-neutrality-hostility patterns among the actors must also be taken into account. Chart 7-2 illustrates three basic divisions among the actors. First, there is the split between local and state governmental units with the former being extremely suspicious of the latter.

*We are speaking figuratively, of course. There is as yet no definitive evidence from ethological or biological research that conclusively proves that any members of *homo sapiens* are actually born with instinctive PRINCE capabilities. See, however, "Nature vs. Nurture and PRINCE: Evidence from Planarian Earthworms and College Sophomores," *American PRINCE Science Review* 2 (September 1971): 80-96.

CHART 7-1. Issue position, salience, and power for improving building productivity in Los Angeles.

Actor	Issue position	Salience	Power	Total for each actor
Housing Department	+3	3	1	+9
Governor	+1	1	2	+2
Mayor of Los Angeles	+1	1	3	+3
Building industry	-1	3	2	-6
Labor	-2	3	3	-18
Consumer	+3	1	1	+3
			Total for the issue	-7

CHART 7-2. Friendship-neutrality-hostility chart.

This actor	Housing department	Governor	Mayor of Los Angeles	Building industry	Labor	Consumer
Housing department	X	-	+	+	+	+
Governor	+	X	-	+	-	+
Mayor of Los Angeles	-	-	X	+	+	+
Building industry	-	+	+	X	-	+
Labor	-	-	-	-	X	-
Consumer	+	-	+	-	-	X

(header spanning: "Feels about this actor")

Second, there is the split between the private groups and the government. This split more clearly involves the Housing Department against business and labor rather than the governor's and mayor's office. Third, there is hostility between the building industry and labor.

Everything Planter did was designed to force the building industry and labor unions to alter their positions through political pressure from the state government. The plan to get the governor to take a firm public stand, to use the state legislature to shape the behavior of business and labor through coercion (uniform laws) and bribes (training grants) and the use of a consumer-dominated watchdog committee were highly visible and straightforward methods to change the way houses were built.

What Planter failed to understand was that the state government had neither the power nor the salience to do very much. Nor could he realistically expect a consumer revolt or even a significant consumer pressure campaign to occur. Moreover, given the hostility of the mayor's office, labor, and the building industry to governmental intervention from the state, Planter's plan could only increase antagonism.

The consequence of Planter's ideas would have been to bring business and labor together in alliance with the local governmental officials to resist the efforts of the Housing Department. The use of high-salience techniques would have created conditions under which business and labor would have forgotten their basic antagonisms and joined together. Nor could there have been much increase in the strength among consumer groups and the governor's office. Given the political structure portrayed in the charts, there was little hope that a coalition among the Department of Housing, the governor, the mayor, and the consumer could have formed or been effective. The governor, the Housing Department head, and members of the state legislature were well versed in the PRINCE system, so it is not surprising that Planter could not get them to accept his strategy for action.

In contrast, LaStrange clearly understood the constraints imposed by limited salience or power for those actors other than the building industry and the labor unions. His understanding led him to devise a strategy that gave the two powerful forces sufficient representation on a committee that was clearly low-profile. A thorough study of the committee illustrates LaStrange's strategy. First, the length of the name of the commission along with the inclusion of such innocuous items as "Ad Hoc" and "Housing and Other Construction" and "Southern California" served further to insure that its activities would be kept on the back pages of the local newspapers. In fact, LaStrange kept the profile so low that the news media never reported much of anything that the committee was doing.

Although people make fun of the jargon and ponderous ways of the bureaucrats, it is the bureaucrats who often have the last laugh. Jargon is like a coat of armor protecting them from politicians and the public so that they can get things done. In this particular case LaStrange's use of such a long title for the committee helped to keep the salience of business and labor low because the rank and file people never really figured out what the committee was supposed to be doing.

PRINCiple 7.7: Bureaucrats use jargon and committees for the political purpose of keeping salience low.

With the low-profile approach, LaStrange was able to get greater cooperation out of the mayor's office and at the same time help to highlight business and labor's differences over the uses of more productive housing technologies. Because they had no fears of being forced or

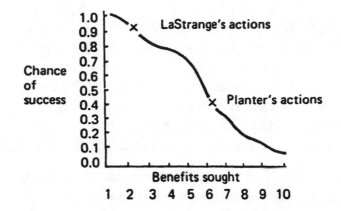

FIGURE 7-1. Relationship between probability of success and benefits sought in getting higher productivity in housing in the Los Angeles area.

bribed to do anything, labor and business never developed the coalition under LaStrange's strategy that they would have under Planter's. At this point, the intrusion of new information via the film presented by the vice-president of Kwiki Homes, Inc. had a maximum effect. It helped to change the attitudes of the two most powerful groups—business and labor—so they were willing to sponsor a moderate proposal for the adoption of new techniques. Once the representative from the mayor's office saw this happening, he cooperated by helping to change some of the building codes in the Los Angeles area.

It is clear that Planter ignored or did not understand the PRINCE method of solving political problems, and it is equally clear that LaStrange did. The final question that must be raised is whether or not we think LaStrange could have achieved any more than he did. If politics is the art of the possible, it is the responsibility of those using the PRINCE system to achieve the maximum, given the limits of feasibility. Did LaStrange settle for too little?

The problem can be illustrated by looking at the position of Planter and LaStrange on the graph appearing in Figure 7-1. That graph shows in the particular example we have used how the chances of success are related to the benefits sought. Notice that the more you seek, the smaller are your chances of success. It is completely analogous to horse racing, where you may bet on long odds and have a small chance of winning a lot of money, or bet on short odds and have a good chance of winning a small amount.* The two "x's" in Figure 7-1 mark the level of benefits sought and the chances of success for LaStrange and Planter. The former played it safe while the latter shot for the moon and achieved no results. The question is whether or not LaStrange could have shot

---

*This is not to imply that the PRINCE system has yet been completely adapted for use in betting on horse races.

for more benefits (represented on a 1-10 scale) without appreciably lowering his chances of getting some success. The way the curve is drawn suggests that he could have. It flattens out between benefits of 2 and 5, which means that the chances of success don't drop very much. Conversely, if Planter had shot for a 5 instead of an 8, he would have increased his chances of success 100 percent.

PRINCiple 7.8: One must always match the chances of success of various alternatives with the relative benefits that would result from the success.

Even so, we should not be too critical of LaStrange. It is even more difficult to draw correctly a line for this kind of graph than it is to fill out the PRINCE charts. There are ways of translating the numbers in the PRINCE accounting system to the graph represented in Figure 7-1, but that involves a course called "The Advance Dynamics of the PRINCE Accounting System and Related Ideas in Political Problem Solving." Very few people have received this kind of training and LaStrange was not one of them. We must understand and even excuse his failure to use this graph. When compared to Planter, LaStrange wins hands down.

Nevertheless, there is a tendency for bureaucrats to pick benefits that do not take advantage of the proper mixture of maximum gain with minimum chance of failure. Generally speaking, we advise that the actor choose benefits when no less than a .5 chance of success is indicated. A .500 batting average in politics would be as spectacular as a .500 batting average in the American League. Bureaucrats tend to pick goals for which there is greater than .8 chance of succeeding. This is why most people think they are losers—their victories are almost always insignificant. Our advice based on the PRINCE system is that bureaucrats should continue to avoid the self-destructive impulses of a Bobby Planter but try to be a little bit more daring than a Mortimer LaStrange. To do this adequately, however, they will have to enroll in the advance course mentioned above.

STUDY 3: THE PRINCE PAPERS AND THE DECISION TO ESCALATE THE VIETNAM WAR

*I*n the summer of 1971, the *New York Times* and other newspapers were receiving effusive congratulations for their daring decision to risk government wrath by printing excerpts from what has come to be called the Pentagon Papers, the detailed study of the United States government's decision-making process concerning the Vietnam War. Much of this praise is undoubtedly deserved. However, even the *New York Times* is human, which is to say subject to fears, doubts, and occasional failure of nerve. In the book-length compilation of the Pentagon Papers, the *Times* editors mention that they did not have access to the complete Pentagon study. What was missing, said the *Times*-men in their misleading but understandable euphemism, were the documents and narrative relating to the "secret diplomacy of the Johnson period." (*The Pentagon Papers* [New York: Bantam Books, Inc., 1971], p. xix).

It can now be told that the contents of the nonreported documents contained much more than the report of a few furtive remarks from one diplomat to another over cocktails in some out-of-the-way capital. The most critical aspects of those documents were some relatively brief copies of communications between members of the Johnson administration and a consulting firm, PRINCEtitute, Inc. **The *Times*** may not have reported these communications because it did not actually get ahold of them, or because even its courageous editors may have feared publicizing the powerful new tool which the administration leaders had at their disposal (and ultimately misused).

We do know that PRINCEtitute, Inc. was as eager as the government to keep these particular documents from public view. In the first place, the firm has become quite embarrassed over its attempt to aid the government's Vietnam adventures. It has directed its attention to peace-related activities, a current project being a study of employing napalm as a barbecue fire-starter. Of equal importance in the mutual desire to supress the PRINCE papers is that the PRINCE system was used so ineptly, and for such dubious moral purposes.

However, in accordance with the notion that full disclosure, no matter how shocking or momentarily embarrassing to the government, is for the public good, we report on these pages what little information we have concerning the attempt to use the PRINCE system to guide American foreign policy in Vietnam. Unfortunately, efforts to prevent the acquisition of information have resulted in our obtaining only a small sample of the relevant documents. Hopefully, it will provide enough of an insight into how the PRINCE system was employed in the Vietnam decision.

Our purpose is not merely to provide such an insight but also to show how the PRINCE system is morally neutral. It can say no more about the desirability of action taken within its framework than an accountant's balance sheet indicates the moral purposes of the organization whose finances he is balancing. Implicitly, we are supposing that there are more good people than bad people. We hope that the spread of PRINCE technology will result in a net benefit to mankind. At the very least, the following fragmentary notes should provide a warning that the PRINCE system can produce wicked policies and long-run failures.

No doubt many people (perhaps even some at the PRINCEtitute) are happy that in this case the PRINCE system helped to contribute to long-run failure. From the vantage point of 1972, everyone, from the president all the way down to the man in the street and even members of the State Department, feel that the Vietnam War was a serious blunder on the part of the United States.

Of course, it was not always so viewed. During the early 1960's, many influential leaders within and outside the government felt that the United States was embarked upon a course that was not only moral, but prudent and feasible. Within this optimistic context, during the middle 1960s, PRINCEtitute, Inc. was brought in as an outside consultant. Although we have no comprehensive account of how the firm influenced the Vietnam decisions, we can piece together statements from the well-known Pentagon Papers as published by the *New York Times* and Bantam Books (quotations are referenced by page numbers of the Bantam edition), memoranda and other communications between members of the Johnson administration and the staff of the PRINCEtitute, and internal documents among members of the PRINCEtitute staff.

By the middle of the 1960s there had developed among President Johnson's advisors a strong consensus that the war against the Communist revolution in South Vietnam was going very badly. The limited-risk, limited-commitment assumptions that had been guiding American foreign policy were becoming less acceptable as the force of events in the field showed their weaknesses. At that point in time, the question of increasing the American commitment had to be dealt with as directly as possible.

Of course many consultants were brought in to help advisors advise the president. Anyone in consultant work knows that his job is to make the kinds of arguments those who hire him expect him to make. Ostensibly, consultants are brought in from outside to bring their objective expertise to bear. In reality, they are introduced into the decision-making process to help their boss carry the day. We have no reason to believe that PRINCEtitute, Inc. was hired for any other purpose. However, we do not know which presidential advisor sought the advice of PRINCEtitute, Inc. in the first place. The only thing we have is the following transcript dated sometime in 1964 of a telephone conversation between PRINCEtitute, Inc. (identified as PRINCE) and a high-ranking White House official (identified as WH). The transcript was edited to remove the Texas accent of the speaker so as to protect his anonymity.

Transcript #1: Sometime in 1964, Between PRINCE and WH

WH: You honestly mean to tell me that you can teach *me* something about dealing with American politics?

PRINCE: I didn't say that, sir. But if you use our system you will be able to more accurately gauge the consequences of whatever policy you decide upon. It seems to me the first thing you should do is to make some estimate of the relative support of the policies you are thinking about carrying out.

WH: I know what public opinion is! Look here, I've got a public opinion poll that shows—

PRINCE: Uh, excuse me, sir. I've seen those confidential polls. Perhaps you forgot that one of your advisors leaked them the other night in an off-the-record briefing on the Dick Cavett Show. Besides that, there are a couple of things wrong with polls for your purposes. In the first place, they tell you how the public felt about a single issue a few weeks ago. They don't say anything about how changes in your position are likely to bring about changed reactions.

WH: But, of course—

PRINCE: And, in the second place; if I may continue, sir, those poll results you talk about show the responses of a sample of the entire population. They don't make any distinctions among various groups of the public. This is especially important when you try to estimate how changing policies will lead to changing public opinion.

The PRINCEtitute staff made several visits to Washington to brief the top-ranking official and his chief advisors in the White House, the State Department, the Defense Department and other parts of the foreign-policy-making establishment. Part of the time was spent explaining the PRINCE system to the officials, and part of the time preparing sets of PRINCE charts for their specific policy interests. On the basis of their conversations, the staff reduced the United States political system to four basic actors and three prominent issues. The actors were the far left, the moderate left, the moderate right, and the far right. The issues were the implementing of civil rights legislation, the passage of measures to fight against poverty, and the escalation of the war by bombing the north and by increasing the number and involvement of American troops. (This last issue was, of course, not yet being widely discussed outside the top circles in government.)

We have the following partial transcript of a talk which occurred in the White House in late summer, 1964.

Transcript #2: In Late Summer of 1964 Between PRINCE and WH

PRINCE: Now that's very good, sir. We have the issue positions and the salience levels for the actors. [*These are reproduced here as Charts 1 and 2.*] Now all we have to do is get together estimates for the power of each actor on each issue and—

WH: Just a god-damned minute! I knew this wasn't going to do me any good. You're going to have us make up one of these little charts for the power on the issues, then multiply the charts together and add the columns to see which of these issues is *really* going to happen, right?

PRINCE: Yes sir, you see—

WH: I sure as hell do see! You're telling me something I don't care about. You think I'm going to set around like a 10-year-old steer in a Juniper patch just waiting to see if these things will happen? They're going to happen because I'm going to *make* them happen! We're going to have more civil rights, more war on poverty, and more commitment to save Vietnam from communism. What I want to know is who's with me and who's against me when I decide to act.

PRINCE: Sir, we don't expect you to just sit idly by and accept the world pictured in the PRINCE charts if you don't—

WH: I told you, I know what I have to do!

PRINCE: Please, sir, let me finish! If you're not concerned about the odds, but just want to count the political costs and benefits, the charts are quite appropriate for that. In fact, all we need are the two charts we have already prepared. What we'll do is multiply the two charts together and add the *rows*, which, as you can see, indicate the combined position and salience for each actor on all three issues. Since these issues are stated in terms of the outcomes which you want to bring about, the higher the score of an actor, the higher its support for the positions you are taking. Here, I'll just multiply—

WH: Never mind! I ain't paying consultants like you $100 an hour to multiply a bunch of numbers. (Speaking into intercom) Marge! Get Walt Rostow over here right away. If he's not around, get Bob MacNamara over here. (Speaking to PRINCE) Would you believe it? I've got these hundreds of geniuses working for me, and Walt and Bob are the only ones who even know how to add two numbers together!

Chart 1

Issues Positions in 1964

	Civil Rights	Poverty War	Vietnam
Left Wing	+3	+3	−3
Liberals	+2	+3	+1
Conservatives	−1	−1	+3
Right Wing	−3	−3	+2

Chart 2

Salience for Issues in 1964

	Civil Rights	Poverty War	Vietnam
Left Wing	3	2	2
Liberals	2	3	2
Conservatives	2	2	2
Right Wing	2	2	3

Through the combined brainpower of the White House and PRINCEtitute staffs, the required multiplication was accomplished, with the results presented in Chart 3.

The next piece of information we have that appears to be relevant are the following lines reproduced from an internal staff memorandum circulated at the PRINCEtitute in early fall, 1964.

PRINCE Internal Memorandum #73:

> ...therefore, a primary conclusion of our PRINCE analysis of the political situation of the Johnson administration is that we have confirmed what the leaders, admittedly, intuitively felt all along: They have a great deal of freedom to maneuver, especially on the issue which concerns them the most, escalation in Vietnam. As can be seen from inspecting display no. Wh-4-32 [*reproduced here as Chart 3*] the ad-

Chart 3

Support of Johnson Policies in 1964

	Civil Rights	*Poverty War*	*Vietnam*	*Total*
Left Wing	+ 100	+ 50	– 80	+ 70
Liberals	+ 40	+ 100	+ 6	+ 146
Conservatives	– 15	– 15	+ 80	+ 50
Right Wing	– 50	– 50	+ 80	– 20

ministration's overall position is supported by all groups except the right wing. Furthermore, the officials of the administration—*including the very highest levels*—believe that increased activity surrounding the Vietnam war will increase salience on that issue for the right wing. This will increase this group's support of the administration without notably decreasing the support of other groups. The moderate and extreme left groups should continue to be favorably impressed with the administration's accomplishments in domestic policy.

What is shaping up, therefore, as we head into the election campaign is a plan to walk a somewhat dangerous—but not overly narrow-tightrope. By continuing the press for domestic reforms in the civil rights and social welfare fields, we—that is the Johnson administration in consultation with the PRINCEtitute—can continue to win support of the liberal and left-wing American political factions. Insofar as we escalate the Vietnam military operations through a carefully orchestrated set of procedures, we can attract favorable attention from the moderately conservative and the right wing. Toward that end we have begun detailed consultation with William Bundy, Assistant Secretary of State for East Asian and Pacific Affairs, on the application of the PRINCE system to the more detailed problem of how to bring about escalation so as to achieve maximum possible support for the policy and for the Administration as a whole.

I hardly need to point out that William Bundy is the brother of McGeorge Bundy, the president's assistant for national security affairs, and one of the most influential men in government. Our success in working with Assistant Secretary Bundy can have important long-run consequences for our

organization's relations with the government. I hope that
the Governmental Liaison Department will take note of this
and undertake appropriate recoding of our own PRINCE
charts vis-á-vis the PRINCEtitute's relations with the government and the prospects for future consultating contracts.

Evidently the hopes expressed in the foregoing memorandum were
easily fulfilled. The following is partial text of a letter from an unnamed
government official to the PRINCEtitute.

**Letter from Someone on the White House staff
to PRINCEtitute, Inc.**

Finally, allow me to thank you for the clear and forceful
presentation of the principles of the PRINCE system. It has
immeasurably assisted me in clarifying my thoughts about
various options to be considered as we adapt our policies in
Southeast Asia to new problems and opportunities. I am sure
that your suggestions will help bring about a set of policy
recommendations which will not only move us toward
our common objectives, but will also receive the support of
people in the United States and throughout the Free World.
You will of course realize the necessity of making some
modifications in the PRINCE system to handle the specifics
of particular policies; I am sure you will agree that the modifications we have made are consistent with the principles
you outlined to me.

Included with this is a document written by Assistant Secretary of
State William Bundy in which he appears to "have sacrificed the rigor of
all the PRINCE charts, (even though) the spirit of PRINCE pervades."
This document which partially reproduced below may be identified as
PRINCEtitute document no. DS-8-13, or as document no. 84 of the *Pentagon Papers,* pp. 363-64.*

*An obvious bit of evidence that Bundy had been influenced by the ideas
of the PRINCE system, which provide for action in all kinds of situations can be
seen from this document's title: "Conditions for Action and Key Actions Surrounding *Any* Decision." (Italics added) The Public Relations Office of the
PRINCEtitute couldn't have put it any better.

Congress must be consulted before any major action, perhaps only by notification if we do a reprisal against another Bien Hoa, but preferably by careful talks with such key leaders as Mansfield, Dirksen, the Speaker, Alabert, Halleck, Fulbright, Hickenlooper, Morgan, Mrs. Bolton, Russell, Saltonstall, Rivers, (Vinson?), Arends, Ford, etc. He probably should wait till his mind is moving clearly in one direction before such a consultation, which would point to some time next week. Query if it should be combined with other topics (budget?) to lessen the heat.

Our international soundings appear to divide as follows:

a. We should probably consult with the U.K., Australia, New Zealand, and possibly Thailand before we reach a decision. We would hope for firm moral support from the U.K. and for participation in at least token form from the others.

b. SEATO as a body should be consulted concurrently with stronger action. We should consult the Philippines a day or so before such action but not necessarily before we have made up our minds.

c. The NATO Council should be notified on the Cuban model, i.e., concurrently by a distinguished representative.

d. For negative reasons, France probably deserves VIP treatment also.

e. In the UN, we must be ready with an immediate affirmative presentation of our rationale to proceed concurrently either with a single reprisal action or with the initiation of a broader course of action.

f. World-wide, we should select reasonably friendly chiefs of state for special treatment seeking their sympathy and support, and should arm all our representatives with the rationale and defense of our action whether individual reprisal or broader.

USIA must be brought into the planning process not later than early next week, so that it it getting the right kind of materials ready for all our information media, on a contingency basis. The same [word illegible] true of CIA's outlets.

The next piece of information we have is a partial transcript of a meeting which took place at the PRINCEtitute offices. The subject of the meeting was to discuss the Bundy statement and to evaluate its consistency with approved PRINCE practices. The conversation recounted below took place between the president of the PRINCEtitute (identified as PRINCE) and a new employee, recipient of a Ph.D. in political science ence from a local university (identified as PHD).

Transcript #3: Discussion Between PRINCE and PHD

PHD: Well, I guess my first question is what is meant by "Bien Hoa." I suppose it's an acronym. . . something like "Building Intelligence and Estimating Networks—"

PRINCE: Just hold it for a minute! You're not in graduate school any more. Stop looking for a hidden meaning in everything. Bien Hoa is an airfield in South Vietnam that was attacked by the Viet Cong last month. Bundy is considering using this attack as a rationale and justification for the escalation which has already been decided upon by the government.

PHD: O.K. Now who are all these guys that Bundy says ought to be talked to? I know that Mike Mansfield is the majority leader in the Senate. . . .

PRINCE: God-damn, if you academics aren't ignorant about American government! Everett Dirksen is the minority leader—he's a Republican incidentally. The Speaker is John McCormack, the top Democrat in the House of Representatives. Carl Albert is the majority leader, the number two Democrat. Charlie Halleck is the Republican minority leader in the House of Representatives.

PHD: I know Fulbright, of course—Chairman of the Senate Foreign Affairs Committee.

PRINCE: Foreign *Relations* Committee, dummy. Didn't you ever learn that it's the House Foreign Affairs Committee and the Senate Foreign Relations Committee? Senators just have relations, they're too old to have affairs.

PHD: You know, I think I've learned more about politics and government in one month here at the PRINCEtitute than three years in graduate school.

PRINCE: I should hope so! Now, Bourke Hickenlooper is the ranking Republican in the Senate Foreign Relations Committee. Thomas Morgan and Mrs. Frances Bolton are the top Democrat and Republican on the House Foreign Affairs Committee. Richard Russell is the chairman of the Senate Armed Services Committee. Leverett Saltonstall is the top Republican on that Committee. Mendell Rivers, Carl Vinson, Leslie Arends, and Walter Norblad are all key members of the House Armed Services Committee.

PHD: Gee, he recommends talking to both Republicans and Democrats. The Johnson Administration really does believe in bipartisanship.

PRINCE: Of course it does. Did you take a good look at those PRINCE charts* that showed the power of the Republicans in Congress, especially the ones who were party leaders or top-ranking committee members? They can cause a lot of heat for the president if they aren't made to feel that they are being consulted.

PHD: What do you mean, "feel" they are being consulted?

PRINCE: Read carefully what he says: "Congress must be consulted. . . only by notification. . . . He (the president) probably should wait till his mind is (made up) before such a consultation." This is an old gimmick, which, to be quite candid, is used as effectively by non-PRINCE players as by PRINCE players. Now let me ask you something. Why do you suppose Bundy suggests talking about the budget at these congressional "consultations"?

PHD: I suppose that's because a meaningful consultation about the escalation of the war would have to include the subject of the costs involved and how the costs should be budgeted.

PRINCE: Come on now! Secretary Bundy is using one of the basic principles of PRINCE calculations—reduce the saliency of an unpopular decision by emphasizing the saliency of other topics. Government spending on domestic programs, the total amount of spending, whether the budget will be balanced—these are the bread-and-butter questions for legislators. If you want to talk about a potentially risky subject, be sure to talk about the budget in the same meetings, and you won't have any trouble. To a congressman the budget is like a cookie jar is to a three-year-old. If you're going to tell your three-year-old something bad—like he can't have a new toy—don't you guide him to the cookie jar while you're telling him?

PHD: We don't have cookies or candy at home, just natural foods.

PRINCE: That figures. But anyway, look at the kinds of actions which PRINCE analysis has suggested to Bundy about international consultation concerning the proposed escalation.

PHD: Yeah, I can see that our legal obligations under the NATO and SEATO treaties—

PRINCE: Legal obligations? That's nothing compared to the obligations tions of rational action implied by PRINCE calculations. Bundy's

*We don't know what was contained in the power charts, since they have never been uncovered.

PRINCE charts concerning the international actors involved in the Vietnam war show that the allies of the United States have the highest salience and power to affect the freedom to maneuver militarily and diplomatically. Therefore the main emphasis has to be devoted to making sure that their issue positions are as close to ours as possible. Bundy has calculated that the foes of the U.S. on this issue can't be changed very much. But their power and salience are rather low anyway, so the goal of warning them is hardly worth the effort.

In point "f", he suggests that friends of the U.S. be initially approached about the shift in policy. You should remember from your American history how George Washington used the PRINCE charts to follow the same basic strategy in achieving consensus on the American constitution.

PHD: I don't remember that from American history.

PRINCE: That's right, you did study history in the old-fashioned way. Anyway, the use of friends by Bundy is just as important. They are not only useful in building support for your policies, of course. But they are also important in helping get exposure of your arguments to actors who may be your enemies, but their friends. Washington used this tactic in spreading pro-constitution propaganda at the Philadelphia convention. I can tell you frankly that we are planning to recommend to the administration that they use the same procedure. We should have, say, England's Prime Minister Harold Wilson argue our case to the Russians. He shares a higher hostility-friendship score with the Russians than we do.*

During this period—from the fall of 1964 onward—nearly every top official was supportive of the proposed escalation, or at least kept silent about his hesitations. They were all engaged with more or less skill in charting alternative ways of moving toward that escalation through use of the PRINCE charts. The PRINCEtitute was closely involved in these activities, monitering and commenting upon the various options and plans advanced by officials in the government.

Unfortunately for President Johnson, his advisors and the American people—not to mention the people of Southeast Asia—the PRINCE-

*Whether because of the PRINCEtitute's recommendations or for other reasons, the Johnson administration did in fact ask Prime Minister Wilson (and, subsequently, other leaders) to take the U.S. case to the Russians.

titute's interest in this project declined sharply. No doubt the official who had initially brought in PRINCEtitute, Inc. thought that the company could be of no more service and started to send his assistants, sub-assistants and on one occasion his secretary, to meet with representatives of the firm. Where the original governmental briefings and communications had been supervised by the top officials of the consulting firm, more and more junior officials of the organization were assigned to the task of checking for the level of PRINCE sophistication in the government plans submitted to PRINCEtitute, Inc. In particular, we have learned that the young employee previously identified as PHD came to exercise actual control over the PRINCEtitute's Vietnam Consulting Project.

Unhappily, PHD was insufficiently confident in the PRINCE system to question what the high level government officials were planning to do. In particular, he was overwhelmed by the attention paid to the letter of PRINCE doctrine, rather than the spirit. That is, he was most concerned that PRINCE charts were correctly filled out, that the issues and actors in any particular analysis did not exceed 3, and so on.

Accordingly, he was led to reject (or rather ignore) analyses which did not conform to the PRINCE format. In retrospect there were two major flaws in PHD's analysis of government documents according to the PRINCE system. Both these errors stemmed from his overriding concern to see that the various PRINCE charts submitted to him were correctly filled out. So long as the charts had some outcomes specified with respect to which issue positions, salience, and power were assigned to the the actors, he was satisfied. He never asked, as a truly skilled PRINCE player should, whether the outcomes specified were actually what the players were concerned about, whether they were feasible goals to try to pursue, and whether the system was including all relevant actors with power to affect the important outcomes.

Memorandum #432: From PHD to White House Staff

> Furthermore, it would seem that the issue is not whether
> it is physically, or even politically, in the short run, feasible
> to engage in an increased military effort in Vietnam. The
> outcomes which are more appropriate have to do with

changing the behavior of the VC (the Vietcong), the DRV
(The Democratic Republic of (North) Vietnam) and for that
matter, the GVN (the Government of [South] Vietnam).
Would it not be reasonable to consider creating PRINCE
charts on the basis of outcomes appropriate to these goals?

In retrospect, it is clear that this question, if pursued, could have
been one of the most profound in the whole decision-making process.
However, PHD was quickly squelched, as so often happens in government, not by rational response, but by the invocation of authority
based on experience. Walter Rostow replied that, of course bombing
was the outcome to be concerned about, since this would bring about
changes in the North Vietnamese policies. Rostow, who had served in
the government during World War II, said, in effect, if it was a good policy then, it's a good policy now.

His response (as printed in *The Pentagon Papers*, p. 499) begins
with a classic introduction to an argument based on simple analogies,
"With an understanding that simple analogies are dangerous. . . ." He
then goes on to say:

I nevertheless feel that it is quite possible the military effects
of a systematic and sustained bombing of POL [petroleum,
oil and lubricants] in North Vietnam may be more prompt
and direct than conventional intelligence [i.e., intelligence
which does not agree with this simple analogy] would sug-
gest.

Had PHD been somewhat more flexible and creative in reading the
documents pertaining to Vietnam which crossed his desk, he might have
realized that he had a potentially successful PRINCE player in the government with whom he could have collaborated. Unfortunately, this official, George Ball, the under-secretary of state, raised objections to the
current drift of policy in non-PRINCE terms. Being a dissident he was
treated as decision-making bodies often treat unpopular spokesmen—he
was excluded from exciting exercises like the PRINCE sessions. Consequently, he raised his objections in terms of cost-benefit analysis. He
did not realize that cost-benefit analysis as a fad had had its day, so he
was doubly out of fashion. The correctness of his analysis could of

course in no degree compensate for the unfashionability of his jargon. PHD, of course, was *au couránt* with the fashionable phrases, so he too ignored Ball's writings, such as the following. Note, in particular, how Ball in July of 1965 stresses the importance of outcomes beyond the immediate decisions to escalate or not; note also that he questions the relative salience of various outcomes, suggesting, that they might be quite low for observers relatively distant from Vietnam. (*The Pentagon Papers*, pp. 449-54).

(2) The Question to Decide: Should we limit our liabilities in South Vietnam and try to find a way out with minimal long-term costs?

The alternative—no matter what we may wish it to be—is almost certainly a protracted war involving an open-ended commitment of U.S. forces, mounting U.S. casualties, no assurance of a satisfactory solution, and a serious danger of escalation at the end of the road.

(3) Need for a Decision Now: So long as our forces are restricted to advising and assisting the South Vietnamese, the struggle will remain a civil war between Asian peoples. Once we deploy substantial numbers of troops in combat it will become a war between the U.S. and a large part of the population of South Vietnam, organized and directed from North Vietnam and backed by the resources of both Moscow and Peiping.

The decision you face now, therefore, is crucial. Once large numbers of U.S. troops are committed to direct combat, they will begin to take heavy casualties in a war they are ill-equipped to fight in a non-cooperative if not downright hostile countryside.

Once we suffer large casualties, we will have started a well-nigh irreversible process. Our involvement will be so great that we cannot—without national humiliation—stop short of achieving our complete objectives. *Of the two possibilities I think humiliation would be more likely than the achievement of our objectives—even after we have paid terrible costs.*

(4) Compromise Solution: Should we commit U.S. manpower and prestige to a terrain so unfavorable as to give a very large advantage to the enemy—or should we seek a

90

compromise settlement which achieves less than our stated
objectives and thus cut our losses while we still have the
freedom of maneuver to do so.

(5) Costs of a Compromise Solution: The answer involves
a judgment as to the cost to the U.S. of such a compromise
settlement in terms of our relations with the countries in
the area of South Vietnam, the credibility of our commitments, and our prestige around the world. In my judgment,
if we act before we commit substantial U.S. troops to combat in South Vietnam we can, by accepting some short-term
costs, avoid what may well be a long-term catastrophe. I believe we tended grossly to exaggerate the costs involved in a
compromise settlement. An appreciation of probable costs
is contained in the attached memorandum.

—With the exception of the nations in Southeast Asia, a
compromise settlement in South Vietnam should not have a
major impact on the credibility of our commitments around
the world . . . Chancellor Erhard has told us privately that
the people of Berlin would be concerned by a compromise
settlement of South Vietnam. But this was hardly an original thought, and I suspect he was telling us what he believed
we would like to hear. After all, the confidence of the West
Berliners will depend more on what they see on the spot
than on [word illegible] news or events halfway around the
world. In my observation, the principal anxiety of our
NATO Allies is that we have become too preoccupied with
an area which seems to them an irrelevance and may be
tempted in neglect to our NATO responsibilities. Moreover,
they have a vested interest in an easier relationship between
Washington and Moscow. By and large, therefore, they will
be inclined to regard a compromise solution in South Vietnam more as a new evidence of American maturity and
judgment than of American loss of face . . . On balance, I
believe we would more seriously undermine the effectiveness of our world leadership by continuing the war and
deepening our involvement than by pursuing a carefully
plotted course toward a compromise solution. In spite of
the number of powers that have—in response to our plead-
ing—given verbal support from feeling of loyalty and de-
pendence, we cannot ignore the fact that the war is vastly
unpopular and that our role in it is perceptively eroding the
respect and confidence with which other nations regard us.

> We have not persuaded either our friends or allies that our
> further involvement is essential to the defense of freedom
> in the cold war. Moreover, the [more] men we deploy in
> the jungles of South Vietnam, the more we contribute to a
> growing world anxiety and mistrust.

There are a number of interesting points about Ball's discussion of the international consequences of withdrawal from Vietnam. Since international consequences were given as the main reason for our policy in the first place, Ball was quite correct in focusing his cost-benefit analysis on that. More importantly, he seems to have intuitively applied the PRINCE system by asking the hypothetical question *What issue position would countries around the world take on certain questions if we pulled out?* In arguing that there would be few changes in those issue positions, Ball was arguing that the costs of the pullout would not be very great and in any case would be less than the costs of remaining in.

But, unfortunately, Ball was alone in raising the cost-benefit issue. To get a policy-making group to consider goals and objectives—which is the essential of the cost-benefit question—when they are busy thinking about how to achieve the objectives, you need more than one man making intellectual arguments. Instead, you need a large number of political actors arguing for a change in policy objectives, which is exactly what happened in 1967 and 1968. Because Ball in the summer of 1965 was willing to accept the convention of maintaining secrecy, he could not search for and develop a political coalition to place the cost-benefit issue on the agenda.

One should not conclude that the Johnson policy-makers were stupid or that Americans never think of ends but always think of means, in spite of the fact that some European intellectuals always accuse the Americans of such behavior. The explanation for the failure to consider questions of goals is quite simple. Human beings order their thoughts in a way that leads them to think about one problem at a time. When you are deciding where to place a nail in a wall in order to hang a picture, you have already decided to hang the picture on the wall. If you are in the process of finding the appropriate spot and you turn to your wife and say "this picture stinks," you have opened up a can of worms—that is, raised a question that your wife thought was already settled. Although such acts of herosim are not unknown in the annals of American husbandry, they take quite a bit of courage and political organization.

Unfortunately, the executive branch of government is not adequately suited for the discussion of cost-benefit issues. The demand for detailed action taken in the atmosphere of secrecy forces a highly structured approach to making decisions. To turn back and deal with questions of general objectives once they have already been discussed is a difficult, if not impossible, task. The answer may be in giving the American Congress more responsibility for these decisions and in using the symbol of national security less freely. Space does not permit the discussion of those questions here. Suffice it to say, those using the PRINCE system in the Johnson regime failed adequately to lay the groundwork for its use by questioning the cost and benefits of the entire policy.

An internal study of the PRINCEtitute, Inc.'s procedure in handling the Vietnam contract was called for in late 1966 when it was discovered that the government had committed en error that even the most juvenile PRINCE player would not commit. The PRINCE system was applied by the government to dealing with the American people and their Congress, American allies (including South Vietnam) and those American neutrals and enemies not directly involved in the war. But it was *not* used in constructing United States' political-military strategy toward North Vietnam and China. The study led to the following memorandum:

PRINCE Internal Memorandum #763: On Contract Failure

Remarks by W. W. Rostow in a letter to Secretary of Defense McNamara on November 16, 1964 (*The Pentagon Papers*, pp. 418-22) have been thoroughly studied. They are reproduced below in parts.

Following on our conversation of last night I am concerned that too much thought is being given to the actual damage we do in the North, not enough thought to the signal we wish to send.

The signal consists of three parts:

a) damage to the North is now to be inflicted because they are violating the 1954 and 1962 accords;

b) we are ready and able to go much further than our initial act of damage;

c) we are ready and able to meet any level of escalation they might mount in response, if they are so minded.

Our most basic problem is, therefore, how to persuade them that a continuation of their present policy will risk major destruction in North Viet Nam; that a preemptive move on the ground as a prelude to negotiation will be met by U.S. strength on the ground; and that Communist China will not be a santuary if it assists North Viet Nam in counter-escalation.

I do not see how, if we adopt this line, we can avoid heightened pressures from our allies for either Chinese Communist entrance into the UN or for a UN offer to the Chinese Communists on some form of two-China basis. This will be livable for the President and the Administration if—but only if—we get a clean resolution of the Laos and South Viet Nam problems. The publication of a good Jordan Report will help pin our allies to the wall on a prior reinstallation of the 1954 and 1962 Accords.

Special analysis of this quote and others reveals that the thinking resembles a mode of thought of Thomas Schelling. An ex-economist, Schelling was the supreme academic advisor of the early 1960's as far as many government officials were concerned. His advice to policy-makers was based in part, on techniques for dealing with his children. From these and other everyday experiences, he suggested that policy-makers should use rewards and punishments to modify behavior.

If PRINCEtitute, Inc. had performed its duties properly, the government, even with people like Rostow running the show, would never have espoused such a simple solution. The problem with the approach of finite rewards and punishments should be clear to anyone, including those who generalize from their experiences with the raising of children or the training of dogs. It is true that you can reward and punish a child to modify his behavior, but only when the salience of the particular issue is sufficiently low. If the salience of what he wants to do is high enough, then such a strategy will not work. If a child has already bragged to his friends that his parents will buy him a laser gun, for example, the promise of a candy orgy will probably not sooth his savage breast, not at least until he can rationalize to his peers why laser guns are no good.

If Rostow and his fellow policy-makers had only looked at the salience charts for North Vietnam and China, they would have been able to tell that increasing the physical punishment on North Vietnam would lead to a stronger, rather than weaker, commitment to fight the South Vietnamese and Americans. They would have also known that Communist China would not trade a seat in the UN for what Rostow calls "a clean resolution of the Laos and South Vietnam problems"—especially with the United States nominating itself as Mr. Clean. It would not be an overestimation to say that China attached ten times more salience to what was going on in Southeast Asia in 1965 than to the opportunity to sit in the UN. (This is especially true since she had good prospects of gaining entry to the UN without toeing the U.S. line.)

What our leaders *should* have done was to construct a PRINCE chart consisting of the political actors within North Vietnam. Rostow correctly understood that there were political actors shaping the policy of North Vietnam—the country was not run by one man. However, if he had constructed a PRINCE system chart, he would have realized that the only way to break the willingness of the country to continue in the battle was to lower the salience of the political future of South Vietnam to the North. The way to do this was not to increase American involvement, but rather to decrease it.

We can only conclude from the study of the Rostow document and other evidence that PRINCEtitute, Inc. performed in a very faulty manner on its Vietnam contract. The worst failure was its inability successfully to oust the Schelling viewpoint from the thinking of those responsible for American foreign policy during the middle 1960s. Equally serious was the inability of the project director to prepare the groundwork properly by getting the right people to issue the contract and to have those in the government openly evaluate the costs and benefits of what they were about to do.

We know who the project director was during the final phases of the contract. It was PHD, and the personnel system of PRINCEtitute, Inc. seems to be working well because Mr. PHD is now a research assistant at CIA. But who the original contract supervisor was seems to be a secret. He must have an awful lot of friends in the company, or maybe a lot of power.

The final communication that we have appeared in a PRINCE memorandum to the White House in 1967. In almost gleeful terms, it outlines the effect of the escalation in Vietnam between 1965 and 1967 on domestic politics within the United States.

Memorandum #1003: From PRINCEtitute, Inc. to the White House Staff

The American policy of escalation appears to have altered both the issue positions and salience of the Liberals and left wing. The right wing and conservatives had also become disenchanted probably because they felt the escalation was not sufficiently high. As Charts 4, 5 and 6 illustrate, in less than three years, Johnson's policies have turned the American political scene from one in which there was basic and overwhelming support for his regime to one in which there was basic and overwhelming opposition.

Multiplying the issue positions and salience registered in 1967, we get Chart 6, which clearly shows Johnson's loss in support when compared with Chart 3. A serious study of the origins of these support figures will reveal that more important than the shift of the actors on issue position towards American policy in Vietnam was the great increase in salience of the Vietnam issue and the decrease in salience of the other issues. As the commitment to Vietnam grew older and greater, the salience of the issue for all groups greatly increased. Once that salience was high, there was nothing Johnson could do to lower it except for removing American troops.

Chart 4

Issue Positions in 1967

	Civil Rights	Poverty War	Vietnam
Left Wing	−1	−2	−3
Liberals	+2	+2	−3
Conservatives	−1	−2	−1
Right Wing	−3	−3	−3

Chart 5

Salience for Issues in 1967

	Civil Rights	Poverty War	Vietnam
Left Wing	2	1	3
Liberals	2	2	3
Conservatives	2	2	3
Right Wing	2	2	3

Chart 6

Support of Johnson Policies in 1967

	Civil Rights	Poverty War	Vietnam	Total
Left Wing	−2	−2	−9	−13
Liberals	+4	−9	−1	− 1
Conservatives	−2	−4	−3	− 9
Right Wing	−6	−6	−9	−21

Unfortunately, we have nothing more to report from the PRINCE papers. Hopefully, the reader can piece together the fragments we have presented and ascertain how the PRINCE system can be misused. Failure to weigh the costs and benefits sufficiently as well as to apply the PRINCE system to all questions of strategy led to failure in Vietnam. It also led to a thorough housecleaning the PRINCEtitute, Inc. Although part of the housecleaning effort was stimulated by the removal of all government contracts involving national security issues from the company, more important was the desire of PRINCEtitute, Inc. to rededicate itself to the mission of making every man a prince.

Some Notable PRINCiples from this Chapter

Don't start using your PRINCE charts until you are sure of your political goals.

Use your political friends to approach those who disagree with you rather than approaching them yourself.

Never forget the spirit of the PRINCE system by becoming bogged down in its procedures.

Secrecy is the way those who favor the consensus maintain it. If you oppose the consensus you must remove the cloak of secrecy so that you can identify your allies.

Stupid ideas capture the minds of governmental officials as easily as smart ideas. The models of the academics are not always harmless or impotent.

Punishing a political group or a society reduces disagreement within that group or society because it raises salience on security issues and simultaneously reduces salience on those issues on which there might be disagreement.

Issue position and salience change much faster than power. Continually update your PRINCE charts.

STUDENT EVALUATION FORM

Title of Learning Package _____Political Analysis through the Prince System_____

Course Title _____ Name of Instructor _____

Specific Parts of Learning Package Which Were Used. (If the whole package was used, please indicate this.)

_____

     This questionnaire is designed to assist your instructor in evaluating the learning package you have just completed. You should answer the questionnaire in terms of that part of the learning package to which you were exposed.
     Circle the letters below which correspond to the response that most nearly agrees with your own. Please be frank as your comments will play a role in helping your instructor as well as the Consortium in improving the package in the future.

1.   All things considered, this learning package was:

    a. excellent   b. good   c. fair   d. poor

2.   To what extent did the learning package help you achieve the stated objectives?

    a. a great deal   b. some   c. little   d. not at all

3.   On the whole, how much do you think you learned as a result of this learning package?

    a. a great deal   b. some   c. not very much   d. nothing

4.   How would you describe your instructor's attitude toward the package?

    a. enthusiastic   b. neutral   c. negative

5.   Please complete the following statement by circling the most appropriate letter after each adjective. When completing the statement, use the following code:
    a = Extremely; b = Very; c = Somewhat; d = Not at all.

I Found This Learning Package to Be:

INTERESTING	a	b	c	d	CHALLENGING	a	b	c	d
BORING	a	b	c	d	A WASTE	a	b	c	d
RELEVANT	a	b	c	d	PRACTICAL	a	b	c	d
INFORMATIVE	a	b	c	d	DEMANDING	a	b	c	d
DIFFICULT	a	b	c	d	DIFFERENT	a	b	c	d
GOOD	a	b	c	d	ENJOYABLE	a	b	c	d
STIMULATING	a	b	c	d	ENLIGHTENING	a	b	c	d
IRRELEVANT	a	b	c	d	EXCITING	a	b	c	d
WORTHWHILE	a	b	c	d	REWARDING	a	b	c	d
VALUABLE	a	b	c	d	PROVOCATIVE	a	b	c	d
NECESSARY	a	b	c	d	GENERAL	a	b	c	d
DULL	a	b	c	d	USELESS	a	b	c	d

6. Listed below are a number of analytical skills which may have been developed as a result of your completing this learning package. By circling the appropriate letter, please indicate the level of competence you felt in each skill before the package was used, and the level of competence you now feel in each skill after having completed the package. Please use the following code: a = A Great Deal; b = Some; c = Little; d = None.

SKILL	BEFORE				AFTER			
	A Great Deal	Some	Little	None	A Great Deal	Some	Little	None
Identify Political Issues the Prince System Can Help You Understand	a	b	c	d	a	b	c	d
Determine Needed Information to Make a Political Forecast about any Issue	a	b	c	d	a	b	c	d
Calculate Probabilities that a Political Decision Will Be Taken	a	b	c	d	a	b	c	d
Identify Strategies to Change Probabilities in Desired Direction	a	b	c	d	a	b	c	d

7. In the space provided, please list the specific ways in which the learning package could be improved.

8. In the space provided, please list those exercises in the learning package which you felt were of little value and indicate how they might be improved.